MISTAKE AND NON-DISCLOSURE OF FACTS

MISTAKE AND NON-DISCLOSURE OF FACTS
Models for English Contract Law

HUGH BEALE

OXFORD
UNIVERSITY PRESS

OXFORD
UNIVERSITY PRESS

Great Clarendon Street, Oxford, OX2 6DP,
United Kingdom

Oxford University Press is a department of the University of Oxford.
It furthers the University's objective of excellence in research, scholarship,
and education by publishing worldwide. Oxford is a registered trade mark of
Oxford University Press in the UK and in certain other countries

© H. Beale 2012

The moral rights of the author have been asserted

First Edition published in 2012

Impression: 1

Crown copyright material is reproduced under Class License
Number C01P0000148 with the permission of OPSI
and the Queen's Printer for Scotland

British Library Cataloguing in Publication Data
Data available

Library of Congress Cataloging in Publication Data
Library of Congress Control Number: 2012941349

ISBN 978–0–19–959388–0

Printed in Great Britain by
CPI Group (UK) Ltd, Croydon, CR0 4YY

Preface

This book is an updated version of the Clarendon Lectures that I gave in November 2009. It was a great honour to be invited to give the Clarendon Lectures, and I am very grateful to the University of Oxford and Oxford University Press, which sponsored the lectures, for the opportunity to discuss in a public forum issues that, as I explain in the first chapter, have concerned me for some time.

One issue is whether English law on mistake and non-disclosure of facts in contracts is in need of reform. The current law is highly individualistic, allowing one party to take deliberate advantage of the other's mistake or ignorance in a way that sometimes seems unjust and inefficient. Some parties can be expected to look after their own interests in all circumstances, but I will argue that this is not always an appropriate approach. The other issue is whether, if it is concluded that change is needed for at least some types of contract, it would be better to amend the current English law or to allow parties who would prefer some protection against mistake and non-disclosure to choose a less rigorous regime of contract law. The European Commission has proposed an 'optional instrument' for contracts within Europe which could form the basis for just such a development.

From this point of view, the book appears at an exciting moment. The European institutions and Member States are currently considering the European Commission's proposal for a Common European Sales Law. This would, in effect, insert into the law of every Member State a second regime of contract law that the parties could choose to apply to cross-border contracts of sale and related services, and for the download of digital content, where the contract is between a business and a consumer or between two businesses where one business is a small or medium-sized enterprise (SME). Member States would have the option to allow the use of the Common European Sales Law for purely domestic contracts and also when neither business is an SME. In terms of substance, the proposed law would have a very different character to current English contract law, in particular in the way it treats mistake and non-disclosure of facts. In the third chapter I argue that the current rule is suitable for the typical commercial contract disputes which form so much of the case-load of the English courts, and therefore we may not want to alter our 'domestic' law. A better way forward might be to provide an alternative, less individualistic regime for those, SMEs particularly, who may want it. This is just what the proposed Common European Sales Law would allow us to do.

My aim is not to present final conclusions on either issue; it is to stimulate debate on the way in which English contract law and contract law across Europe might be developed. As I explain in the first chapter, the book is intended to work rather like a Law Commission Consultation Paper, making provisional proposals and seeking responses.

Partly for that reason, I have tried to preserve the spirit of the original lectures. I have included a small amount of material that I did not mention in the lectures for want of time, and have provided basic references in the footnotes, but I have not tried to expand it into the full treatise that could be written on the topic.

In particular, the material on the way mistake and non-disclosure of facts is handled in other legal systems is not a full comparative treatment. There are two reasons for this, one good and one not so good. The good reason is to keep it short and easy to read. The other is that for many of the continental laws—in particular, Dutch law, German law, and the 'Nordic' laws—I have had to work from the primary and secondary sources that are available in English. Some of these seem excellent—I would like to commend particularly the second edition of *The German Law of Contract* by Markesinis, Unberath, and Johnston. I would also like to thank colleagues and research assistants who have helped me to find information and who have often corrected my misunderstandings. I cannot name them all but I would like to give particular thanks to Timothy Dodsworth and Gillian Murdoch (University of Warwick) and Dr Jacobien Rutgers (Free University of Amsterdam). Mistakes remain my own; and even though this is a case in which the mistaken party must bear the risk, I hope that colleagues who are better informed will point out to me where I have gone wrong. Some readers may remain uncomfortable that I have not been able to check all the original sources for myself. The only justification I can give is that when we think how many languages there are in Europe, let alone the rest of the world, a process of trial and error of this kind seems to be the only way to develop and use what we can learn from other legal systems.

Hugh Beale
April 2012

Contents

Table of Cases   xi
Table of Instruments and Legislation   xix
Abbreviations of Frequently Cited Material   xxiii

1. Defining the Issues   1
   Background: 'European' principles of
      contract law   3
   Defining the issue   14
   Real differences between the English and
      'European' laws   19
   Conclusions   26

2. Mistake and Non-Disclosure in Other Systems   33
   Commonwealth laws   33
   European models   42
   United States   68
   What to make of this survey   71

3. Possible Models for English Law   75
   Models not to follow   76
   The underlying aim: protection of autonomy
      or fairness in exchange?   77
   A plausible 'informed consent' model   78
   Remedies   95
   Should the rules be mandatory?   97
   A provisional proposal   98
   Do we want to adopt this kind of model?   99

Appendix   125
Index   135

Table of Cases

COMMON LAW CASES

Australia

Blomley v Ryan (1956) 99 CLR 395, 402 36
Commercial Bank of Australia v Amadio (1983)
    151 CLR 447 (H Ct) 23
Crowe v Commonwealth Bank of Australia [2005]
    NSWCA 41 36
Demagogue Pty Ltd v Ramensky (1992)
    110 ALR 608 34–5
Elkofari v Permanent Trustee [2002] NSWCA 413 36
Groeneveld Australia Pty Ltd v Nolten 2010
    VSC 533 (unrep, 2010) 35
Mikaelian v Commonwealth Scientific and
    Industrial Research Organisation (1999)
    163 ALR 172 35
Miller & Associates Insurance Broking Pty
    Ltd v BMW Australia Finance Ltd (2010)
    270 ALR 204 (H Ct) 35
Taylor v Johnston (1983) 151 CLR 522 (H Ct) 33
Walford v Miles [1992] 2 AC 128, 138 104

Canada

Ames v InvestoPlan Ltd (1973) 35 DLR (3d) 613 36
Belle River Community Arena Inc v Kaufmann
    (1978) 87 DLR (3d) 761 (Ont SC)....................... 37
Calgary (City) v Northern Construction Co (1982)
    23 Alta LR (2d) 338 (QB) 39
Imperial Glass Ltd v Consolidated Supplies Ltd
    (1960), 22 DLR (2d) 759 (B.C. Court of Appeal) 37
McGrath v MacLean (1975) 95 DLR (3d) 144 37
McMaster University v Wilchar Construction Ltd
    22 DLR (3d) 9 (Ont SC)...................................... 37

MJB Enterprises Ltd v Defence Construction
    (1951) Ltd 170 DLR (4th) 577 (SCC) 38
R v Ron Engineering & Construction (Eastern)
    Ltd (1981) 119 DLR (3d) 267 38
Radhakrishnan v University of Calgary Faculty
    Association (2002) 215 DLR (4th) 624 (Alta CA) 36
Ryan v Moore 2005 SCC 38, 254 DLR (4th) 1 36
Toronto Transit Commission v Gottardo
    Construction Ltd (2005) 257 DLR (4th) 539 38–9
Ward v Cudmore (1987) 75 NBR (2d) 112 (QB) 37

New Zealand

Janus Nominees Ltd v Fairhall CA 336/2008,
    [2009] 3 NZLR 757 40
Kings v Williamson (1994) 2 NZ ConvC 95, 234 41
Ladstone Holdings Ltd v Leonora Holdings
    Ltd CP 308/SD00, [2006] 1 NZLR 211 (H Ct) 39
New Zealand Refining Co Ltd v Attorney-General
    (1992) 14 NZTC 9,006 (Greig J) 39
New Zealand Refining Co Ltd v Attorney-General
    (1993) 15 NZTC 10,038 (CA) 39
Tri-star Customs & Forwarding Ltd v Denning
    [1999] 1 NZLR 33, 37 40
Vaucluse Holdings Ltd v NZ Guardian Trust Ltd
    [2000] CA 237/99 40

Singapore

Chwee Kin Keong v Digilandmall.com Pte
    Ltd [2005] SGCA 2, [2005] 1 SLR 502 .... 15, 33

United Kingdom

4Eng Ltd v Harper [2008] EWHC 915 (Ch),
    [2009] Ch. 91 80
Amiri Flight Authority v BAE Systems
    Plc [2003] EWCA Civ 1447 101
AXA Sun Life Services plc v Campbell Martin Ltd
    [2011] EWCA Civ 133, [2011] 2 Lloyd's Rep. 1 108

Bank of Credit and Commerce International
   SA (In Liquidation) v Ali (No. 1) [2001]
   UKHL 8, [2002] 1 AC 251 .... 23, 109, 123
Brennan v Bolt Burdon [2004] EWCA Civ
   1017, [2005] QB 303 .... 30, 98
British Bankers Association, Re v Financial Services
   Authority [2011] EWHC 999 (Admin), [2011]
   Bus. LR 1531 24
Bunge Corp v Tradax Export SA [1981] 1 WLR 711 104
Centrovincial Estates Plc v Merchant Investors
   Assurance Co Ltd [1983] Com. LR 158 80
Chartbrook Ltd v Persimmon Homes Ltd [2009]
   UKHL 38, [2009] 1 AC 1101 108–9
Conlon v Simms [2006] EWCA Civ 1749 21
Credit Lyonnais Nederland NV v Burch
   [1997] CLC 95, 101 23
Cresswell v Potter [1978] 1 WLR 255, 257 23
C. Czarnikow Ltd v Koufos or The Heron II
   [1967] UKHL 4 110
Denny v Hancock (1870) LR 6 Ch App 1 .... 41, 70
Derry v Peek (1889) 14 App Cas. 337 57
Do-Buy 925 Ltd v National Westminster
   Bank plc [2010] EWHC 2862 (QB) 101
J. Evans & Son (Portsmouth) Ltd v Andrea
   Merzario Ltd [1976] 1 WLR 1078 108
Fry v Lane (1888) 40 ChD 312 22
Great Peace Shipping Ltd v Tsavliris Salvage
   (International) Ltd [2002] EWCA Civ 1407,
   [2003] QB 679 33
Greaves & Co (Contractors) Ltd v Baynham Miekle
   & Partners [1975] 1 WLR 1095 22
Grogan v Robin Meredith Plant Hire (1996)
   15 Tr LR 371, CA 101
Halpern v Halpern [2007] EWCA Civ 291,
   [2007] 2 Lloyd's Rep. 56 6
Hartog v Colin and Shields [1939] 3 All ER 566 ...... 2, 15, 37
HIH Casualty and General Insurance Ltd v
   Chase Manhattan Bank [2003] UKHL 6, [2003]
   2 Lloyd's Rep. 61 97

HIH Casualty & General Insurance Ltd v New
Hampshire Insurance Company Independent
Insurance Company Ltd [2001] EWCA Civ 735,
[2001] 2 Lloyd's Rep. 161.................................. 101
Hong Kong Fir Shipping Co Ltd v Kawasaki
Kisen Kaisha Ltd [1962] 2 QB 26..................... 108
IFE Fund SA v Goldman Sachs International
[2006] EWHC 2887 (Comm), [2007] 1
Lloyd's Rep. 26 59
IFE Fund SA v Goldman Sachs International
[2007] EWCA Civ 811, [2007] 2 Lloyd's Rep. 449........ 59
Interfoto Picture Library Ltd v Stiletto Visual
Programmes Ltd [1989] QB 433, CA 101
Investors Compensation Scheme Ltd v West
Bromwich Building Society [1998] 1 WLR 896.......... 109
Jackson v Union Marine Insurance Co (1874)
LR 10 CP 125 111
Kleinwort Benson Ltd v Lincoln City Council
[1999] 2 AC 349.. 98
L'Estrange v Graucob Ltd [1934] 2 KB 394..................... 101
Levett v Barclays Bank plc [1995] 1 WLR 1260 21
Livesey v Jenkins [1985] AC 424 21
Mannai Investment Co Ltd v Eagle Star Life
Assurance Co Ltd [1997] AC 749..................... 109
Malins v Freeman (1837) 2 Keen 25, 34–5 41
Metropolitan Water Board v Dick, Kerr &
Co [1918] AC 119... 111
Musawi v RE International (UK) Ltd [2007]
EWHC 2981 (Ch), [2008] 1 Lloyd's Rep. 326.......... 6
North Shore Ventures Ltd v Anstead Holdings
Inc [2011] EWCA Civ 230, [2011] 3 WLR 628 21
Ocean Chemical Transport Inc v Exnor Craggs
Ltd [2000] 1 Lloyd's Rep. 446, 454..................... 101
Pan Atlantic Insurance Co Ltd v Pine Top
Insurance Co Ltd [1995] 1 AC 501 20
Parabola Investments Ltd v Browallia Cal
Ltd [2009] EWHC 901 (Comm) 80
S. Pearson & Son Ltd v Dublin Corp [1907] AC 351......... 97

Peekay Intermark Ltd v Australia & New Zealand
    Banking Group Ltd [2006] EWCA Civ 386, [2006]
    2 Lloyd's Rep. 511 108
Phillips v Homfray (1871) 6 Ch App 770, 780 21
Prenn v Simmonds [1971] 1 WLR 1381 109
Redgrave v Hurd (1881) 20 ChD 1, CA 102
Ruxley Electronics and Construction Ltd v
    Forsyth [1996] AC 344 103
Smith v Hughes (1871)
    LR 6 QB 597 .... 16–18, 30, 36, 41, 107
Springwell Navigation Corp v JP Morgan
    Chase Bank [2010] EWCA Civ 1221,
    [2010] 2 CLC 705 108
Statoil ASA v Louis Dreyfus Energy Services
    LP [2008] EWHC 2257 (Comm), [2008] 2 Lloyd's
    Rep. 685 (The Harriette N) 1–2, 15–16, 29, 75, 81–2
Sykes v Taylor-Rose [2004] EWCA Civ 299,
    [2004] 2 P & CR 30 .... 27, 71, 75
Tate v Williamson (1866) 2 Ch App 55 21
Thake v Maurice [1986] QB 644 22
Transfield Shipping Inc v Mercator Shipping Inc
    [2008] UKHL 48, [2009] 1 AC 61 109
Turkey v Awadh [2005] EWCA Civ 382,
    [2005] 2 FCR 7 29
Walker v Boyle [1982] 1 WLR 495 25
William Sindall plc v Cambridgeshire CC
    [1994] 1 WLR 1016, CA 95
Williams v Roffey Bros & Nicholls (Contractors)
    Ltd [1991] 1 QB 1 108–9
Winterton Constructions Pty Ltd v Hambros
    Australia Ltd (1992) 111 ALR 649, 666 35
Wood v Scarth (1855) 2 K&J 33, 3 Eq Rep 385 41
Wood v Scarth (1858) 1 F&F 293 41

United States of America

AMPAT/Midwest v Illinois Tool Works 896
    F 2d 1035 (7th Cir 1990) 71
Beatty v Depue, 103 NW 2d 187 (SD 1960) 70

Blair v National Security Insurance Co 126
    F 2d 955, 958 (3d Cir 1942) 73
Board of Regents of Murray State Normal
    School v Cole, 273 SW 508 (Ky 1925) 69
Boise Junior College District v Mattefs Construction
    Co, 450 P 2d 604 69
Centex Construction Co v James, 374 F 2d 921
    (8th Cir 1967) 69
Crenshaw County Hospital Board v St Paul Fire
    and Marine Insurance Co, 411 F 2d 213
    (5th Cir 1969) 69
Geremia v Boyarsky, 140 A 749 (Conn 1928) 69
Laidlaw v Organ 15 US (2 Wheat.) 178
    (1817) 17, 70–1, 92, 93
Market St Associates v Frey 941 F2d 588
    (7th Cir 1991), 594 91
Obde v Schlemeyer, 353 P.2d 672
    (Wash 1960) 70, 75, 77, 81–2, 91
Reed v King 193 Cal Rptr 130 (Cal Ct App 1983) 71
Ricketts v Pennsylvania Rly Co 153 F 2d 757, 766–7 79
Tony Down Food Co v United States, 530F 2d 367
    (Ct of Claims 1976) 70

NATIONAL CASES

Finland

Supreme Court of Finland, KKO 1949 II 258 66
Supreme Court of Finland, KKO 1968 II 33 67
Supreme Court of Finland, KKO 1975 II 92 66
Supreme Court of Finland, KKO 1985 II 58 66

France

Cass civ, 23 November 1931, DP1932.1.129,
    ann Josserand; Gaz Pal 1932.1.96 43
Cass civ, 29 November 1968, Gaz Pal 1969. II.63 46
Pig Farm case, Cass civ 3, 2 October 1974,
    Bull civ III.330; D1974, IR.252; RGLJ 1975.569 .... 46, 88
Poussin case, Cass civ, 3.2.1981, D. 1984.J.49747

Cass civ 13 December 1983,
    JCP 1984.II.20186 ....3–4, 43–4, 51, 61–2, 88
Poussin case, Cour d'appel, Versailles,
    7 January 1987 .... 61–2, 88
Cass 1 civ, 24 March 1987, D. 1987.488.............. 43–4, 45, 51
Cass civ 3e, 17 January 2007, D., 2007, 1051, note
    D. Mazeaud, et 1054, note Ph. Stoffel-Munck............. 51
RTD civ, 2007, 335, obs J. Mestre et B. Fages.................... 51
Defrénois 2007, 443, obs E. Savaux 51
RDC 2007/3, 703, obs Y. M. Laithier 51
JCP 2007, éd. G, II, 10042, note Ch. Jamin...................... 51
Cont conc conso 2007, no. 117, obs L. Leveneur................ 51

Germany

RG 7 December 1911, RGZ 78, 239...................................... 56
RG 5 April 1922, RGZ 104, 265 56
BGH 18 December 1954, BGHZ 16, 54 54
BGH 10 July 1970, LM § 276 [Fa] BGB No. 34,
    NJW 1970.1840 56
BGH 25 May 1977, BGHZ 69, 53 57
BGH 31 January 1979, LM § 123 BGB
    Nr 52....................................1–3, 29, 56, 58–60, 75–6
BGH 3 March 1982, NJW 1982, 1386................................ 58
BGH NJWRR 1988, 394 58
BGH 8 June 1988, BGH NJW 1988, 2597 54
BGH 13 July 1988, NJW 1989.763 59
BGH NJW 1993, 1703.. 58
BGH NJW 1995, 1549.. 58
BGH 6 December 1996, BGH NJW-RR 1996, 429........... 58–9
BGH NJW 2001, 2163.. 58
BGH 28 February 2002, BGH NJW 2002, 2312 54
BGH NJW 2003, 2381.. 58

The Netherlands

Stevensweerd Kantharos, HR 19 June 1959.................... 61–2
HR 10 April 1998, NJ 1998, 666.. 63
HR 14 November 2008, NJ 2008, 588 63

Sweden

Swedish Supreme Court, NJA 1975.152 67
Swedish Supreme Court, NJA 1981.894 65

Table of Instruments and Legislation

CIVIL CODES

Dutch Civil Code (Burgerlijk Wetboek), 1992

Art. 6:162 63
Art. 6:228 .... 61–2, 85, 133
Art. 6:228(1)(b) 62
Art. 6:228(2) 61

French Civil Code *(Code civil)*, 1804

Art. 1109 131
Art. 1110 131
Art. 1110(1) 43

German Civil Code *(Bürgerliches Gesetzbuch)*, 1900

§ 119 .... 60, 72, 132
§ 119(1) 52, 80
§ 119(2) 53–5, 57
§ 121(1) 52
§ 122 .... 46, 55, 60, 72, 79, 80, 132
§ 123 .... 55, 75
§ 142 52
§ 143 52
§ 242 56
§ 305 100
§ 306 17
§ 307 101–2
§ 307(2) 102
§ 307(3) 102
§§ 307–309 102
§ 434 58

NATIONAL LEGISLATION

Australia

Australian Consumer Law 2011
s 18(1) 34
s 236 34
s 237 34
Competition and Consumer Act 2010
s 18(1) 34
Federal Trade Practices Act 1974
s 52 34
Trade Practices Act 1974
s 52 34–5
s 52(1) 34

Denmark

Danish Sale of Goods Act (2003) 65
§ 76(1)(iii) 65
Nordic Contracts Act (1916) 64, 72, 76–7, 133
Art. 1 66
§ 32 64
§ 33 ..... 66–8, 76, 106, 133

§ 36..............67–8, 76, 133
§ 39..................................68

Finland

Finnish Sale of Goods Act
    (1987)
    § 19.................................65
Nordic Contracts Act
    (1929) ... 64, 72, 76–7, 133
    Art. 1 66
    § 32.................................64
    § 33..... 66–8, 76, 106, 133
    § 36..............67–8, 76, 133
    § 39.................................68

Germany

Standard Terms of Business
    (AGBG) Act
    (1976)...........................100

India

Indian Contracts Act 1872
    s 17.................................34
    s 18.................................34

Malaysia

Malaysian Contracts Act
    1950...............................34

New Zealand

Contractual Mistakes Act
    1977.....................39, 76–7
    s 4...................................40
    s 6.............................130–1
    s 6(1)(b)(i) 40, 77
    s 6(1)(c)......................40–1
Contractual Remedies Act
    1979

s 6....................................39
s 7....................................39

Norway

Nordic Contracts
    Act (1918)............. 64, 72,
                        76–7, 133
    Art. 1 66
    § 32.................................64
    § 33..... 66–8, 76, 106, 133
    § 36..............67–8, 76, 133
    § 39.................................68
Norwegian Sale of Property
    Act (1992)
    §§ 3–7 65

Sweden

Nordic Contracts
    Act (1915)............. 64, 72,
                        76–7, 133
    Art. 1 66
    § 32.................................64
    § 33..... 66–8, 76, 106, 133
    § 36..............67–8, 76, 133
    § 39.................................68
Swedish Land Code (1970)
    § 19.................................65

United Kingdom

Arbitration Act 1996
    s 46(1)(b) 6
Consumer Insurance
    (Disclosure and
    Representations) Act
    2012
    s 2..............................20–1
    s 12(2) 21
Equality Act 2010............. 91

Financial Services and
Markets Act 2000 21
s 150 24
Home Information Pack
(Suspension)
Order 2010, SI
2010/1455 25
Housing Act 2004
s 162 25
Marine Insurance Act 1906
s 18 20
Matrimonial Causes Act
1973
s 25 21
Misrepresentation Act 1967

s 3 97
Sale of Goods Act 1979 .. 26,
84
s 14(2) 21
s 14(2)(c) 21
s 14(3) 21
Unfair Contract Terms Act
1977 .... 101–2, 116
s 7(3) 105
s 26 116
s 27 116
Unfair Terms in Consumer
Contracts
Regulations 1999, SI
1999/2083 .... 101, 117

Abbreviations of Frequently Cited Material

Asser-Hartkamp	A Hartkamp & C Sieburgh, *Asser's handleiding tot de beoefening van het Nederlands burgerlicht recht, Verbintenissenrecht* (Kluwer, Deventer, 2010)
CESL	European Commission, Proposal for a Regulation of the European Parliament and of the Council on a Common European Sales Law, 11 October 2011 COM(2011) 635 final.
Chitty	H Beale (Gen ed), *Chitty on Contracts* (30th edn, Sweet & Maxwell, London, 2008).
DCFR	C von Bar and E Clive (eds), *Principles, Definitions and Model Rules of European Private Law: Draft Common Frame of Reference* (OUP, Oxford and Sellier, Munich, 2009); also available in an Outline Edition (Sellier, Munich, 2009), containing the Introduction and articles.
Farnsworth	A Farnsworth, *Contracts* (4th edn, Aspen, New York, 2004).
Kramer, IECL	E Kramer and T Probst, 'Defects in the Contracting Process', in *International Encyclopedia of Comparative Law*, Vol VII, *Contracts in General* (Möhr Siebeck, Tübingen, 2001).
Ius Commune casebook	H Beale, B Fauvarque-Cosson, J Rutgers, D Tallon, and S Vogenauer (eds), *Ius Commune Casebooks for the*

	Common Law of Europe: Cases, materials and text on Contract Law (2nd edn, Hart, Oxford, 2010).
Malaurie	P Malaurie, L Aynès, and P Stoffel-Munck, *Les obligations* (5th edn, Paris: Répertoire Defrénois, 2011).
Markesinis	B Markesinis, H Unberath, and A Johnston, *The German Law of Contract* (2nd edn, Hart, Oxford, 2006).
Munch K	Münchener Kommentar zum Bürgerlichen Gesetzbuch (6th edn, Beck, Munich, 2012).
Nicholas	B Nicholas, *The French Law of Contract* (2nd edn, Clarendon Press, Oxford, 1992).
PECL	*Principles of European Contract Law, Parts I and II* (ed O Lando and H Beale) (Kluwer, The Hague, 2000) (PECL Pts I & II); *Part III* (ed O Lando, E Clive, A Prüm, and R Zimmermann) (Kluwer, The Hague, 2003) (PECL Pt III).
Restatement 2d	American Law Institute, *Restatement of the Law Second, Contracts 2d* (American Law Institute, St Paul, 1981).
Rome I Regulation	Regulation (EC) No 593/2008 of the European Parliament and of the Council of 17 June 2008 on the law applicable to contractual obligations.
Sefton-Green	R Sefton-Green (ed), *Mistake, Fraud and Duties to Inform in European Contract Law* (CUP, Cambridge, 2005).
Terré	F Terré, P Simler, Y Lequette, *Les obligations* (10th edn, Dalloz, Paris, 2009).

Treitel

E Peel (ed), *Treitel, The Law of Contract* (13th edn, Sweet & Maxwell, London, 2011).

UPICC

UNIDROIT, *Principles of International Commercial Contracts* (3rd edn, Unidroit, Rome, 2010).

Zimmermann, *Obligations*

R Zimmermann, *The Law of Obligations: Roman Foundations of the Civilian Tradition* (Juta, Cape Town, 1990; OUP, Oxford, 1996).

1

Defining the Issues

The issues that I want to address in the three chapters of this book can be typified by two cases, one English and one German. The English case is *The Harriette N*,[1] decided in 2008. The parties agreed a compromise on the amount of demurrage (compensation for delays in unloading a ship) that the buyers should pay the sellers, who were liable to the owners. The buyers knew that the sellers were conducting the negotiations on the basis that the ship had completed unloading by a certain date when in fact it was not completed until significantly later, but the buyers decided to say nothing.

In the German case,[2] the claimants and the defendant had made an agreement under which the right to exploit a film series called *Daktari* was transferred to the claimants, but if any German TV company were to take a licence to show the film, the defendants would receive 50 per cent of the earnings. Later the defendant offered to sell back this right to a share of the profit for a lump sum of $10,000. The claimants accepted this offer without revealing that, shortly before, they had received an offer from a German TV company to pay DM 8.3m for the rights, which meant that the defendant's rights were worth much more than $10,000. The defendant purported to avoid the contract for fraud; the claimants sought a declaration that the agreement was binding.

In the German case, the Federal Court of Justice, the *Bundesgerichtshof* (BGH), held that, in the circumstances

---

[1] *Statoil ASA v Louis Dreyfus Energy Services LP (The Harriette N)* [2008] EWHC 2257 (Comm), [2008] 2 Lloyd's Rep. 685.

[2] BGH 31 January 1979, LM § 123 BGB Nr 52 (trans Markesinis case no 92).

of the case, the claimants had a duty to disclose the TV company's offer and their failure to do so might amount to fraud. In the English case, however, the court held that the settlement was binding; the mistake was simply irrelevant.[3] Relief is not given because one party has made a mistake about the facts underlying the contract, even if the other party is fully aware both of the fact that the mistake has been made and that the mistaken party would never have made the contract had they known the truth.[4] The law's attitude is that parties should make full enquires before entering contracts and, if they do not, they have only themselves to blame.

The main question I want to address is whether English law is right to take this individualist attitude, or whether it should move towards the German position, which is broadly representative of most continental legal systems. But I am also going to argue that our answer as to English Law may affect how we should approach another question: whether within Europe we want to develop a so-called 'Optional Instrument', often described as a 28th (or, in deference to the Scots, 29th)[5] law of contract, which parties could choose to use to govern their contract instead of it being governed by one of the domestic national laws.

---

[3] However, the sellers' claim for the full amount of demurrage succeeded because the settlement concluded on the mistaken basis had been superseded by a second agreement under which the buyers had agreed to pay in full.

[4] It was not a term of the contract that discharge was completed on the date the claimant supposed: [2008] EWHC 2257 (Comm) at [91]. (If the mistake had been as to one of the terms, the buyers would not have been able to 'snap up' the apparent offer when they knew that it did not represent the seller's intended offer: *Hartog v Colin and Shields* [1939] 3 All ER 566.) There is no equitable jurisdiction to set the contract aside: [2008] EWHC 2257 (Comm) at [105].

[5] Though we will see that the form of Optional Instrument being proposed by the European Commission is more accurately described as a second system within the law of each Member State: below, p 9.

BACKGROUND: 'EUROPEAN' PRINCIPLES OF CONTRACT LAW

Over the last 15 years, there have been numerous attempts to state principles of contract law for use within Europe or internationally. At the international level we have the *Unidroit Principles of International Commercial Contracts* (UPICC).[6] Within Europe, we have a draft European Contract Code[7] produced by the Academy of European Private Lawyers (often known as the Gandolfi group, after its founder[8]); and we have the *Principles of European Contract Law*[9] (the PECL or 'Lando Principles'). There has also been an attempt to state the principles which underlie the 'European contract law' emerging from the various Directives and the decisions of the Court of Justice of the EU (the 'Acquis Principles').[10] The PECL, with some changes, have been combined with the Acquis Principles[11] to form Books I–III of the *Draft Common Frame of Reference*[12] (DCFR) produced jointly by the Acquis Group and the Study Group on a European Civil Code (SGECC). The PECL have also been used by the SGECC as the basis for restatements on

---

[6] Now in a third edition (2010).

[7] G Gandolfi (ed), *Code Europeén des contrats: avant-projet* (Giuffrè, Milan, 2007). The English text is reprinted in O Radley-Gardner, H Beale, R Zimmermann and R Schulze (eds), *Fundamental Texts on European Private Law* (Hart, Oxford, 2003), 439.

[8] An account of the organization may be found at <http://ec.europa.eu/consumers/cons_int/safe_shop/fair_bus_pract/cont_law/stakeholders/5-20.pdf>.

[9] See *Principles of European Contract Law, Parts I and II* (PECL Pts I & II); *Part III* (PECL Pt III).

[10] Research Group on the Existing EC Private Law, *Contract I: pre-contractual obligations, conclusion of contract, unfair terms* (Sellier, Munich, 2007); see also *Common Frame of Reference and Existing EC Contract Law* (2nd revised edn by R Schulze, Sellier, Munich, 2009).

[11] Thus the DCFR contains a number of provisions applying only to consumer contracts, whereas the PECL do not make special provision for consumer contracts: PECL Pts I & II, Introduction, p xxv.

[12] Study Group on a European Civil Code and Research Group on EC Private Law (Acquis Group), *Principles, Definitions and Model Rules of European Private Law, Outline Edition* (Sellier, Munich, 2009); complete edition (six volumes) (Sellier, Munich and OUP, Oxford) (DCFR).

specific contracts. These have been published separately[13] but are also to be found in the DCFR. Meanwhile, the French Association Henri Capitant and the Société de Legislation Comparée have produced proposals for a revised version of the PECL.[14]

All these groups purport to set out principles which are already shared by most Member States or which are found in international conventions—or at least principles which the relevant group believes should be acceptable to parties within the EU or internationally for use in transnational contracts.[15]

I say 'which are shared or should be acceptable' because it cannot be claimed that the PECL or the other sets of principles always represent common ground. If you adopt the so-called 'functional approach', stripping out as far as possible all the differences in terminology and concepts used in the different laws of contract and concentrating on the result that each system would reach on a concrete set of facts, there is a surprising amount in common between the various laws of contract. I will give some examples later. To that extent, it may be correct to refer to these sets of principles as 'restatements'. On some issues, however, there are undoubted differences even in the concrete results, some of them quite extreme. This means that when the PECL or the UPICC suggest a rule or principle to govern the situation, it can represent no more than what the majority of the group considered to be the 'best solution'— or an acceptable compromise.

---

[13] In series of volumes each entitled Study Group on a European Civil Code, *Principles of European Law—Sales* (etc) (Sellier).
[14] B Fauvarque-Cosson and D Mazeaud (eds), *European Contract Law—Materials for a Common Frame of Reference: Terminology, Guiding Principles, Model Rules* (Sellier, Munich, 2008).
[15] Thus the Introduction to the PECL states that 'The Commission on European Contract Law has...drawn in some measure on the legal systems of every Member State...[but] it has not confined its sources to the national laws of the Member States. It has drawn on a wide range of legal materials from both within and outside Europe, including the American Uniform Commercial Code and Restatements' (PECL Pts I & II, pp xxv–xxvi).

The purposes of these sets of principles vary between projects and between the members of each group. Some participants see them principally as academic exercises in comparative law. At the other extreme, other members of the same group think of them as first drafts for a single European law of contract[16] or even a European civil code.[17] Two further purposes for the principles of contract were, I believe, shared by almost all members of the Lando group and the Study Group. These are that the principles—the PECL or many of the principles drafted by the Study Group:

(1) could be used by contracting parties who are in different states and who do not want their contract to be governed by either party's national law (perhaps because each was unfamiliar with the other's contract law, or thought some aspect of it to be unsuitable for their purposes); and

(2) could be used as a model for development of the laws of contract of the Member States, whether by legislation or case law.

As to the first of these uses, as things stand, any contract must be governed by a national system of law. One draft of the Rome I Regulation on the law applicable to contractual relations[18] would have permitted the parties to adopt 'rules of the substantive law of contract recognised internationally' in place of a national law,[19] but this idea was dropped, possibly in part because of the difficulty of defining what principles are 'recognised internationally'. The result is that parties cannot have their contract governed by the PECL or

---

[16] 'Ultimately the Member States may wish to harmonise their contract law. The Principles can serve as a model on which harmonisation work may be based': (PECL Pts I & II, p xxiv).

[17] The Introduction to Study Group on a European Civil Code, *Principles of European Law—Sales* (Sellier, Munich, 2008), vii, written by Professor Dr Christian von Bar, describes the Study Group as the successor to the Commission on European Contract Law.

[18] See now Regulation (EC) No 593/2008 of 17 June 2008 on the law applicable to contractual obligations (Rome I Regulation).

[19] Brussels, 15.12.2005; COM (2005) 650 final (2005/0261 (COD)), art 3(2).

the UPICC. However, they can adopt the principles as part of their contract,[20] and for some purposes this will achieve something close to the same result. This is because in many systems, including English and Scots law, for business to business (B2B) contracts there are relatively few 'mandatory' rules which the parties cannot exclude or alter. Most of the law consists of 'dispositive' or 'default' rules which apply only so far as the parties have not agreed otherwise. So if the parties agree that the PECL or UPICC are to form part of their contract, the effect will be to replace much of national law by the principles.

Secondly, many laws allow clauses under which disputes are to be subject to arbitration not according to national law but on broader principles such as 'internationally accepted principles of commerce'.[21] The PECL and UPICC both state that they may be applied by arbitrators as modern statements of accepted principle, or may be adopted expressly by the parties.[22]

With the European Commission's *Action Plan* on European Contract Law[23] and its call for a Common Frame of Reference (CFR),[24] two new purposes for 'Restatements' were added. First, the CFR should form a legislator's guide or 'toolbox' to provide fundamental principles, definitions and model rules. These would assist in the revision of existing EC legislation[25] and the drafting of any new harmonizing measures. Discussion of the usefulness or

---

[20] Rome I Regulation, Recital (13).

[21] For English law see Arbitration Act 1996, s 46(1)(b); *Halpern v Halpern* [2007] EWCA Civ 291, [2007] 2 Lloyd's Rep. 56 at [38]; *Musawi v RE International (UK) Ltd* [2007] EWHC 2981 (Ch), [2008] 1 Lloyd's Rep. 326 at [82].

[22] PECL art 1:101(2) and (3); UPICC Preamble.

[23] *Action Plan on A More Coherent European Contract Law* COM (2003) final, OJ C 63/1 (AP); *European Contract Law and the revision of the acquis: the way forward*, COM(2004) 651 final, 11 October 2004 (WF). There is a very large literature on the Commission's plans. A good though critical introduction is S Whittaker, 'A framework of principle for European Contract Law?' (2009) 125 LQR 616.

[24] AP, para 72.

[25] Eight directives were to be reviewed: WF, p 3. The Directives to be reviewed were 85/577 ('Door-step Selling'), 90/314 ('Package Travel'),

otherwise of the CFR as toolbox is outside the scope of this book.[26] Secondly, the CFR might form the basis of an Optional Instrument if it were decided that one was desirable to enable parties within Europe, and particularly parties in different Member States wishing to make cross-border transactions, to operate on the basis of a shared law of contract, at least for the issues covered by the Optional Instrument.[27]

When the lectures on which this book is based were given in November 2009, it seemed that if there was to be any official (or 'political'[28]) CFR, anything to be adopted in the near future was likely to be no more than a toolbox;[29] any Optional Instrument seemed to be some years away. However, the position changed very rapidly after responsibility for the CFR project was transferred from the Directorate-General for Health and Consumer Affairs to the Directorate-General for Justice. In July 2010 the European Commission published a Green Paper setting out various options.[30] These ranged from doing nothing, through creating a CFR toolbox in various forms, a Recommendation to Member States on contract law, or an Optional Instrument to, at the extreme, a harmonizing Directive on European contract law and even a full-blown European Civil Code.

93/13 ('Unfair Terms'), 94/47 ('Timeshare'), 97/7 ('Distance selling'), 98/6 ('Unit prices'), 98/27 ('Injunctions') and 99/44 ('Consumer sales').

[26] I have set out my understanding of the purpose and function of the CFR as a toolbox in H Beale, 'The Future of the Common Frame of Reference' (2007) 3 *European Review of Contract Law* 257, 261–265.

[27] WF para 2.1.2. There was to be 'further reflection' on the need for an Optional Instrument: see AP, especially paras 89–97 and WF para 2.3.

[28] For the distinction between the 'academic' DCFR and a narrower 'political' CFR, see DCFR, Introduction, paras 1, 4 and 6.

[29] This seemed to be the majority position in the European Council: Council of the European Union, Justice and Home Affairs, 18 April 2008, 8397/08 (Presse 96), p 18. See also H Beale, 'The Content of the Political CFR—How to Prioritise' in J Kleineman (ed), *A Common Frame of Reference for European Contract Law* (Stockholm Centre for Commercial Law, 2011) 27, 28.

[30] Green Paper from the Commission on policy options for progress towards a European Contract Law for consumers and businesses, Brussels, 1 July 2010, COM (2010) 348 final.

Not all the options seemed to be serious candidates—the UK Government would never agree, for example, to full harmonization of contract law, let alone a European Civil Code. The front runners seemed to be the CFR as a toolbox and the Optional Instrument—options which could co-exist.

Meanwhile in April 2010 the Commission established a group of experts charged to turn parts of the DCFR into an Optional Instrument.[31] As the Commission did not know what the CFR would be, the Group was asked to draft on an 'as if' basis—which seemed to mean as if an Optional Instrument were required. The Expert Group was, in effect, asked to draft a model Optional Instrument to see if the idea can be made workable.[32] The draft was initially to cover cross-border sales contracts between businesses and consumers (B2C) and between businesses (B2B). Later, the scope was expanded to cover 'related services' such as installation and maintenance. The Expert Group's draft was published in May 2011, as a 'Feasibility Study'.[33] In October the Commission made a formal proposal for a Regulation on a Common European Sales Law.[34] In broad terms the proposed Common European Sales Law (CESL), which is contained in an Annex to the draft Regulation, follows the Expert Group's draft. However it has been expanded to

[31] Commission Decision of 26 April 2010 setting up the Expert Group on a Common Frame of Reference in the area of European contract law (2010/233/EU).

[32] The Expert Group was told to not to concern itself with a toolbox, though this was said to be not because the toolbox idea had been dropped. Subsequently, however, the Commissioner has referred to the Feasibility Study (see next note) as the toolbox (Keynote Speech at the Conference 'Towards a European Contract Law' co-organized by the Study Centre for Consumer Law of the Catholic University of Leuven and the Centre for European Private Law of the University of Münster); others have called the DCFR a sufficient toolbox (see <http://www.law.ed.ac.uk/epln/blogentry.aspx?blogentryref=8781>).

[33] See *A European contract law for consumers and businesses: Publication of the results of the feasibility study carried out by the Expert Group on European contract law for stakeholders' and legal practitioners' feedback* (May 2011) (available at <http://ec.europa.eu/justice/contract/files/feasibility_study_final.pdf>.

[34] Proposal for a Regulation on a Common European Sales Law, 11 October 2011 COM (2011) 635 final.

include downloads of digital content, while some issues covered by the Expert Group's draft have been omitted[35] and there have been numerous minor changes of drafting and substance.

At the technical level, the proposed CESL would work rather like the Vienna Convention on the International Sale of Goods (CISG) does at present. In those states which have ratified the CISG and brought its rules into force, the CISG forms part of the national law, but a part which applies only to international sales contracts of the relevant types and then only if the parties have not opted out. Similarly, the CESL would form part of the law of each Member State, and parties could opt to use it at least for cross-border contracts either within the EU or, if the contract is B2B, where one of the parties has its habitual residence in a Member State.[36] So, like the CISG, within its scope of application the CESL would displace the 'domestic' national law. Issues that are not covered by the CESL—such as the authority of agents and contracts that are illegal or otherwise contrary to public policy[37]—would be governed by the national law that would otherwise apply under the Rome I Regulation.[38]

But though the CESL would be optional in the sense that the parties would be able to choose whether or not to use it, at least in a B2C contract the parties would not be free to exclude certain parts of it.[39] Their contract would either be governed by the CESL or by the domestic national law. Whichever system applied, some of the rules would remain dispositive and to that extent the parties' freedom would

---

[35] e.g. art 27, Negotiations contrary to good faith and fair dealing (cf PECL art 2:301; DCFR art II.–3:301).

[36] Proposed reg art 4(2). For the purposes of the Regulation, the habitual residence of a company is its place of central administration; that of a trader who is a natural person, that person's principal place of business (proposed reg art 4(4)). Member States may opt to allow its use also for contracts which are not cross-border: proposed reg 13(a). On this see further below, p 121.

[37] See Recital 27 of the proposed regulation.

[38] i.e. the law chosen by the parties under art 3 or the law determined under art 4 of the Rome I Regulation.

[39] Art 8(3) of the draft regulation.

not be affected. But just like any national law, the CESL would contain many mandatory consumer protection rules. It aims to provide 'a high level of consumer protection'.[40] This is seen as an essential element of the CESL. At present, a consumer who deals with a business that trades in the country of the consumer's habitual residence or that 'directs such activities' towards that country is entitled to the protection of the mandatory rules of that country.[41] If the parties opt to use the CESL, the 'domestic' national law will be displaced by the provisions of the CESL, so the CESL must provide consumers with adequate protection.[42]

For B2B contracts the position is different. First, most of the provisions of the CESL are 'default rules' which are designed merely to fill gaps in the parties' agreement, and which can be excluded by contrary provision. Like domestic national laws the CESL does contain a number of mandatory rules applicable to B2B contracts.[43] However, as the proposed Regulation is currently drafted, in a B2B contract the parties may opt for it to apply only in part, which seems[44] to have the effect that the mandatory rules can be

---

[40] See Recital 11 and art 1 of the proposed regulation.

[41] Rome I Regulation, art 6(2).

[42] As the CESL will form part of the law of each Member State, art 6(2) of the Rome I Regulation never comes into play. See Recital 12 of the proposed Regulation.

[43] e.g. art 2 (Good faith and fair dealing); art 56 (Remedies for fraud, threat and unfair exploitation); art 70 (Duty to raise awareness of not individually negotiated contract terms); art 74 (Determination of price); art 81 (Provisions on unfair terms); art 171 (Interest for late payment); art 186 (Agreements concerning prescription).

[44] The intended position for B2B contracts is not wholly clear. Commission Officials have said publicly that the parties would not be free to exclude the mandatory provisions of the CESL. However, art 8(3) implies that in a B2B contract the parties can choose that only part of the CESL will apply to their contract. The articles which make various rules of the CESL mandatory are contained in the relevant chapters of the CESL: e.g. CESL art 81, which prevents the parties from excluding the application of the Chapter on Unfair terms or derogating from or varying its effects, is contained in Chapter 8, Unfair contract terms. So it seems that a choice under art 8(3) that a particular chapter of the CESL should not apply will be effective to exclude even the mandatory rules of the chapter.

avoided—though the parties will then be subject to the rules of the otherwise applicable national law.

The proposed CESL is contentious. There are many issues which I will not address, such as how we could ensure uniformity of interpretation and application: whether this could be achieved through supervision by the Court of Justice in its current form aided by the sharing of information and principles of comity, or whether, in order to get decisions quickly and cheaply, we would need to develop a special lower tribunal for European contract law cases. Nor will I discuss the vexed question of whether there is a legal base for the adoption of any Optional Instrument.[45] What I will argue in Chapter 3 is that our attitude towards whether we should agree to adopt the CESL, and possibly in the future to pursue a wider Optional Instrument, may be affected by what we want to do or do not want to do about domestic English contract law.

I would like to add here a few words about the use of the PECL and the UPICC as models for developing contract law. They have been quite influential in the newer democracies in Central Europe and some of the Baltic States, many of which have revised or are in the process of revising their laws of contract or their civil codes. The Principles have not necessarily been followed but they have been much discussed and we are told that they have had a significant influence.[46]

The PECL have also had some influence in western European jurisdictions, though at first this seemed to be in a

---

[45] The proposal claims to be based on art 114, Treaty on the Functioning of the European Union: Explanatory Memorandum, p 8. See the interesting study by S Weatherill and S Vogenauer, 'The European Community's Competence for a Comprehensive Harmonisation of Contract Law—an Empirical Analysis' (2005) European LR 821.

[46] See the collection of essays, 'European Initiatives (CFR) and Reform of Civil Law in New Member States' in (2008) XIV *Iuridica International*, especially: I Kull, 'Reform of Contract Law in Estonia: Influences of Harmonisation of European Private Law', ibid, 122; A Kisfaludi, 'The Influence of Harmonisation of Private Law on the Development of the Civil Law in Hungary', ibid, 130; J Rajski, 'European Initiatives and Reform of Civil Law in Poland', ibid, 151.

reverse sense. In France, the *Avant-projet Catala* (2005) for a major updating of the Code civil[47] was a counter-reaction in response to a perceived threat from European models, whether in the form of harmonization or of a single European law of contracts.[48] Catala's response was primarily to update the Code civil so as to reflect modern case law.[49] Some of its provisions were possibly influenced by European models. But ideas for reform are being carried forward by another a group of scholars set up by Professor François Terré[50] and by the Ministère de Justice.[51] Both the Terré draft and the Ministry's so-called 'Chancellerie' drafts definitely show signs of influence by the PECL and the UPICC.[52]

To turn to English law, however deep the differences between our law and those of our continental neighbours, in many concrete cases English law reaches much the same result as the majority of other Member States. It is impossible to put a figure on the degree of correspondence but if we were to count it by 'chapters of the book', I would guess that for some three-quarters of the time we would be describing broadly similar outcomes. However, there are a few areas where our law and the laws of our continental neighbours are fundamentally different, and possibly the greatest of

---

[47] P Catala, *Avant-projet de réforme du droit des obligations et de la pre-scription* (La Documentation française, Paris, 2006). See J Cartwright, S Vogenauer and S Whittaker (eds), *Reforming the French Law of Obligations: Comparative Observations on the Avant-projet de réforme du droit des obligations et de la prescription* (Hart, Oxford, 2009); and the special issue of *Revue des contrats* 2006/1.

[48] See Cartwright et al (n 47) and the references cited there.

[49] Ius Commune casebook, 79.

[50] F Terré (ed), *Pour une réforme du droit des contrats* (Dalloz, Paris, 2009).

[51] Ministère de la Justice, *Projet de réforme du droit des contrats* (July 2008) and *Projet de réforme du droit des contrats* (May 2009), which is available at <http://droit.wester.ouisse.free.fr/textes/TD_contrats/projet_contrats_mai_2009.pdf>. See the special issue of *Revue des contrats* 2009/1.

[52] See Ius Commune casebook, 80; R Sefton-Green, 'The DCFR, the *Avant-projet Catala* and French Legal Scholars: A Story of Cat and Mouse?' (2008) 12 Edinburgh LR 351.

these differences is over mistakes as to facts and non-disclosure.

I am not arguing that we should necessarily adopt a continental model. However, if English law is completely out of line with European models, I think it is appropriate for us to review English law to see whether after all it is best suited to modern needs. The case for review is stronger if other common law jurisdictions are also moving away from the English model. When I was a member of the Law Commission, it was agreed by the Law Commission and the (then) Lord Chancellor's Department that there was a case for reviewing areas of English contract law which appear to be substantially different to the 'European norm' as represented by the PECL. As a result, a project to look at the area of mistake and non-disclosure in contract law was included in the Law Commission's 9th Programme of Work.[53] But the Law Commission had to give priority to more urgent and more politically visible projects such as insurance and consumer law, and mistake was put forward only for possible inclusion in the 10th Programme.[54] When the 10th Programme appeared,[55] there was no reference to it. But I agree with what John Cartwright said in his Inaugural Lecture at the University of Leiden:[56] the debate should be held. If the issue seems too remote for the Law Commission, the debate should be organized by academics. If academic analysis and other contributions to the debate suggest there is a convincing case for change, it can be raised again with the Law Commission or directly with Government.

---

[53] See Law Commission, *Ninth Programme of Law Reform* (Law Com No 293, 2005), paras 4.12–4.22. The topic of a duty to disclose in sales of land had been considered by the Conveyancing Standing Committee in 1988–1990, see further below, p 28.

[54] Ibid, para 4.22.

[55] Law Commission, *Tenth Programme of Law Reform* (Law Com No 311, 2008). Nor is there any mention of it in the Eleventh Programme (Law Com No 330, 2011).

[56] J Cartwright, 'The English Law of Contract: Time for Review?' (2009) 17 European Review of Private Law 155.

So my topic is this: how does English law on mistake and non-disclosure of facts in contracts differ from other European models, and is it right to do so; or should we consider some reform of English law?

Later I will argue that this is not just a technical question, nor can we treat the law of mistake in isolation. It raises more fundamental issues about the underlying policy or philosophy of our contract law and the kind of contract law we want. What I hope to show is that there is a convincing case for some change. However, I will argue that it need not take the form of change to English law. Instead we may want to make a different law available in the form of an Optional Instrument. We may want to move away from thinking about systems of contract law as 'national' or 'for transnational contracts', towards a notion that parties should have a choice between differing models, geared towards different purposes and differing attitudes towards legal risk.

In this chapter I will describe the provisions on mistake and non-disclosure of fact found in the PECL, compare them to English law and ask where the differences really lie in practice. In Chapter 2, I will look at a selection of other laws of contract, in particular at models found in national systems which supposedly form the basis of the PECL provisions. Then in the last chapter I will ask two questions. First, if we are interested in considering an alternative model, what model would be the best, or at least what choices are there? In other words, I will try to develop an equivalent to the Law Commission's 'provisional proposal'. The second question is: what kind of contract law do we want?

In this book I will not have space to explore every aspect of the subject which would need to be considered. However, I hope to set out the principal options and to start the debate.

DEFINING THE ISSUE

To lawyers, the word 'mistake' already has overtones as to what is relevant and in particular, what in a given system is not 'legally relevant'. I will take a functional approach, seeking to define the problem I wish to address in terms of the facts. It is the situation where one party (let me refer to him as the claimant C) has made the contract in a mistaken belief about the nature of the subject-matter or the surrounding facts. C may have a positive belief which is incorrect; or it may be that it has not occurred to him that the facts are not as assumed. The mistake is not shared by the other party (let me refer to her as the defendant D), however; nor is the mistake the result of anything said or any positive thing done by D. D has at most 'acquiesced in C's mistake'.

This excludes a number of typical 'mistake' cases. First, it excludes mistakes about what terms are being agreed: both mutual misunderstanding and 'mistakes in the offer being made' (as in the recent case involving British Airways in the US, in which BA's website mistakenly offered flights to India for \$40 when what BA had meant to do was to add \$40 to the existing price of over \$800[57]). We all know that if C has made a mistake in its offer and D knows this, D cannot 'snap up' the offer.[58] Arguably this area of the law also needs reviewing, but I will mention it only to point up the complete contrast to the result in *The Harriette N*.[59] In that case the mistake was not about the terms of the offer itself—the figure at which the sellers were prepared to settle—but was in the underlying assumptions; and the

---

[57] Reported in *The Guardian*, 9 October 2009. 'It was later reported that BA offered \$300 to fliers who mistakenly booked the \$40 fare to India, as it sent out an urgent email to travel agents, "As these fares were so clearly below the normal fare levels, British Airways is unable to honor these bookings. We have cancelled all affected bookings made during this two-hour window and will make a full refund for any paid for and issued ticket." It also said it would refund any fees associated with rebooking other airline segments on the same ticket': see <http://www.tropicpost.com/british-airlines-in-major-goofs/>.

[58] *Hartog v Colin & Shields* [1939] 3 All ER 566; see also *Chwee Kin Keong v Digilandmall.com Pte Ltd* [2005] SGCA 2, [2005] 1 SLR 502, noted by Yeo in (2005) 121 LQR 393 (buyers tried to take advantage of offer on Internet to sell goods at mistakenly low price).

[59] *Statoil ASA v Louis Dreyfus Energy Services LP (The Harriette N)* [2008] EWHC 2257 (Comm), [2008] 2 Lloyd's Rep. 685; above, n 1.

judge held (in line with the classic authority of *Smith v Hughes*[60]) that the mistake was of no legal relevance.[61]

Secondly, it excludes the case in which C's misapprehension was the result of incorrect information provided by D—in other words, cases that we would treat under the rubric of misrepresentation. If D knew the information to be incorrect or that it might well not be correct, most EU systems produce a very similar result: the resulting contract can be avoided for fraud, usually without showing the incorrect information was fundamental, and in addition the victim of the fraud may recover damages in tort.[62] If D was not fraudulent, we are in one of those areas in which different systems produce similar results but on different conceptual bases. Whereas English law provides that the contract may be rescinded on the ground of misrepresentation, most civil law systems (and, as we shall see, the PECL) would deal with this under the heading of mistake, albeit one that was induced by the other party.[63] However, the net result will be much the same: if C's mistake was sufficiently serious, C will have a right to avoid the contract, and if D should have known that the information it was giving was incorrect, C will be entitled to damages.

I am also going to exclude mistaken identity[64] and the case where there was no misrepresentation but the parties shared the same mistaken belief as to the facts—in English law terms, cases of 'common mistake'. I exclude common mistake because again the different systems produce broadly similar results—namely that either party may escape from the contract.[65] It is true that in this type of case,

---

[60] (1871) LR 6 QB 597; see below, pp 17–18.

[61] [2008] EWHC 2257 at [88]–[91].

[62] See the Notes to PECL art 4:107 and to DCFR art II.-7:205.

[63] See the Notes to PECL art 4:103, esp Notes 1 and 3; and Notes to DCFR art II.-7:201, esp Notes 1–2 and 18–24.

[64] Because mistaken identity is closely intertwined with the rules on transfer of property by non-owners it is not feasible to review one without the other. I will be considering whether contracts should be voidable for mistake or non-disclosure, not whether they should be void: see below, p 95, n 65.

[65] PECL art 4:103, Note 4; DCFR art II.-7:201, Note 25.

English law gives relief in far fewer situations than do some continental laws. Particularly after the decision of the Court of Appeal in *The Great Peace*,[66] which said that common mistake applies only if it turns out that the contract or the 'contractual venture' was impossible,[67] a German lawyer might say that English law has no doctrine of common mistake, only one of initial impossibility. Until the reforms to the Bürgerliches Gesetzbuch (BGB), Germany's civil code, in 2001, initial impossibility was covered by a separate provision of the BGB (§ 306 former BGB). But because there is at least some shared ground here, I shall leave common mistake for another occasion—though what we decide should be done in the case of unilateral mistake may affect our view on 'common mistake' cases.

Discussion of cases where C has made a unilateral mistake as to facts, which was not induced by incorrect statements or misleading action by D, has been ongoing for a very long time. Cicero discusses the case of the merchant who takes a cargo of corn to Rhodes, where there is a famine, and sells it at a very high price without revealing his certain knowledge that just over the horizon there is a large fleet of other ships carrying corn.[68] Cicero clearly thinks that the merchant acted immorally but he does not give a clear view on the law. In 1817 the US Supreme Court had to decide *Laidlaw v Organ*.[69] D had bought a large quantity of tobacco at a price which was low since tobacco could not be exported because of the British blockade of New Orleans, without revealing his information that a treaty had been signed and the blockade would be lifted. The court held that the buyer had no obligation to disclose his information. Likewise in the classic English case, *Smith v Hughes*,[70] where the court drew a distinction between the seller knowing that the buyer would only be interested in oats that were

---

[66] *Great Peace Shipping Ltd v Tsavliris Salvage (International) Ltd (The Great Peace)* [2002] EWCA Civ 1407, [2003] QB 679.

[67] [2002] EWCA Civ 1407 at [76].

[68] Cicero, *De officiis* 3.50 and 57.

[69] 15 US (2 Wheat.) 178 (1817).

[70] (1871) LR 6 QB 597.

'warranted' to be last season's oats—when any mistake or disagreement would be over the terms of the proposed contract—and the buyer's mistake being merely as to the facts. If the buyer intended to buy the parcel of oats without a warranty as to their age but in the belief that they were old, his mistake was irrelevant even if it was known to the seller.[71] The same case gives us the example of the mineral deposit under the seller's land, which was used in argument and referred to in the judgments. To quote Cockburn CJ:

The case put [in argument] of the purchase of an estate, in which there is a mine under the surface, but the fact is unknown to the seller, is one in which a man of tender conscience or high honour would be unwilling to take advantage of the ignorance of the seller; but there can be no doubt that the contract for the sale of the estate would be binding.[72]

In all these cases it is assumed that one party knows that the other is labouring under a mistake, and that if the other knew the truth, he would not enter the contract. Later I will also consider the case in which C has made a mistake of this kind but D does not know of C's mistake. But let us stick with the case where D knows of C's mistake—the known mistake. The basic rule of English contract law seems absolutely clear: C has no basis for avoiding the contract. Even if D knows that C would never have entered the contract or anything like it had he known the truth, D is fully entitled to take advantage of the mistake.

The contrast with the PECL could hardly be stronger. Article 4:103 (Fundamental Mistake as to Facts or Law) provides that a party who has entered a contract under a mistake of fact may avoid it provided that

   (a) the other party knew or ought to have known of the mistake, and it was contrary to good faith and fair dealing to leave the mistaken party in error; and

---

[71] See Blackburn J at (1871) LR 6 QB 597, 608 and Hannen J at 610.
[72] (1871) LR 6 QB 597, 604.

    (b) the other party knew or ought to have known that the mistaken party, had it known the truth, would not have entered the contract or would have done so only on fundamentally different terms.[73]

There are two exceptions: where the first party's mistake was inexcusable and where the risk of the mistake was assumed, or in the circumstances should be borne, by the mistaken party. The DCFR provision[74] is much the same; it has been re-drafted to make it clearer but without any change in substance.

The PECL provide more than just a remedy for mistake. If D deliberately failed to point out the mistake, that may amount to fraud. Art 4:107 (Fraud) provides that fraud includes fraudulent non-disclosure of any information which in accordance with good faith and fair dealing D should have disclosed.[75]

Nor is this purely a 'European' approach. The UPICC contain a broadly similar provision,[76] though there are some differences to which I will refer later.[77]

REAL DIFFERENCES BETWEEN THE ENGLISH AND 'EUROPEAN' LAWS

The first question we must consider is whether the contrast between English law and the European models is really as stark as it first appears. We all know that the general rule I have described has many exceptions, when English law, directly or indirectly, does impose a duty to disclose, or prevents a party taking advantage of the other's mistake. We need to look in more detail to see where the real differences lie.

---

[73] The full article is printed in the Appendix of Extracts from principles, legislation and reform proposals, below, p 125.

[74] DCFR art II.–7:201.

[75] Likewise DCFR art II.–7:205.

[76] UPICC 2010 art 3.2.2.

[77] See below, pp 79–80.

The exceptions are well known. They were well described some years ago by Waddams in his essay in honour of Patrick Atiyah[78] and most of them are set out in the leading texts.[79] It would be redundant to go through them in detail, so most of them I will simply list.

In terms of 'direct' duties, we have first the exception for contracts of insurance, where the insured is required to disclose to the insurer any fact that a reasonable insurer would want to know about in deciding whether or not to accept the risk and on what terms.[80] It is true that for retail insurance to consumers and some small businesses, the exception has effectively been reversed again by the combined requirements of the Insurance Conduct of Business Rules issued by the Financial Services Authority and the requirements of the Financial Ombudsman's Service, which regards an insurer who tries to rely on non-disclosure of some matter that the insurer hasn't asked about as not treating the customer fairly.[81] As a result, an insurer that exercises its legal right to avoid the policy for non-disclosure risks being fined[82] and being made to pay anyway[83]— a wonderful example of joined-up law-making. Fortunately, Parliament has decided to rationalize the situation by abolishing the consumer's duty to disclose material information; when the Consumer Insurance (Disclosure and Representations) Act 2012 is brought into force, the

[78] S Waddams, 'Pre-contractual Duties of Disclosure' in P Cane and J Stapleton (eds), *Essays for Patrick Atiyah* (Clarendon Press, Oxford, 1991), 237.

[79] e.g. Treitel, paras 9–130 *et seq*; M Chen-Wishart, Contract Law (4th edn, OUP, Oxford, 2012), 212–216; E McKendrick, Contract Law (9th edn, Palgrave Macmillan, Basingstoke, 2011), 218–224; Chitty paras 6–142 *et seq*.

[80] Marine Insurance Act 1906, s 18; see *Pan Atlantic Insurance Co Ltd v Pine Top Insurance Co Ltd* [1995] 1 AC 501.

[81] See Law Commission and Scottish Law Commission, *Misrepresentation, Non-disclosure and Breach of Warranty by the Insured* (LC CP No 182, SLC DP No 134, 2007), paras 3.11 *et seq*; and their Report, *Consumer Insurance Law: Pre-contract disclosure and Misrepresentation* (Law Com No 319 and Scot Law Com No 219, 2009), paras 2.34–2.52.

[82] Law Com Report, para 2.38.

[83] Law Com Report, para 2.48.

consumer will merely have a duty to take reasonable care not to make a misrepresentation to the insurer.[84] But for most business insurance contracts the duty to disclose remains firmly in place.

There are also duties of disclosure in some family arrangements[85] and between prospective business partners.[86] Information that has been obtained wrongfully, e.g. about mineral deposits which were discovered only by trespassing on C's land, must be disclosed.[87] There must also be disclosure if the parties are in a relation of trust and confidence.[88] In contracts of suretyship there is a limited duty to point out unusual features of the contracts involved.[89] Under the Financial Services and Markets Act 2000 there are various statutory duties on company promoters and the like.[90]

Other duties are indirect. For example, a supplier acting in the course of a business must supply goods that are of satisfactory quality and, if the customer has made known a particular purpose for which it requires the goods, that are reasonably fit for that purpose.[91] There is an exception, however, for defects of which the customer knows.[92] The effect is that if the supplier is aware of defects which would make the goods unsatisfactory, or of characteristics which make them unsuitable for the customer's purpose, the supplier must reveal them or be liable.

---

[84] Consumer Insurance (Disclosure and Representations) Act 2012, s 2. The section is to come into force on a day to be appointed, s 12(2).

[85] See Matrimonial Causes Act 1973, s 25 (as amended); *Livesey v Jenkins* [1985] AC 424.

[86] See *Conlon v Simms* [2006] EWCA Civ 1749 at [127].

[87] *Phillips v Homfray* (1871) 6 Ch App 770, 780.

[88] *Tate v Williamson* (1866) 2 Ch App 55.

[89] *Levett v Barclays Bank plc* [1995] 1 WLR 1260; *North Shore Ventures Ltd v Anstead Holdings Inc* [2011] EWCA Civ 230, [2011] 3 WLR 628.

[90] See Treitel, para 9–149; Chitty, paras 6–153–6–154.

[91] Sale of Goods Act 1979, s 14(2) and (3).

[92] s 14(2C). Section 14(3) will not apply if the seller points out that the goods will not do what the buyer wants, as any reliance by the buyer would then be unreasonable.

There is no statutory fitness for purpose requirement for services, but at common law the courts have occasionally reached similar results: if the purchaser of services has specified a particular requirement, the supplier may be under a strict duty to supply services which will fulfil the requirement.[93] Even if the services are not impliedly warranted to produce the result wanted, if the supplier should know that the service to be provided may fail to achieve the desired result, the supplier may be liable in negligence for failing to warn the other party. In *Thake v Maurice*[94] a surgeon was liable for failing to warn a couple that a sterilization operation on the husband might reverse itself naturally. I think the same must apply when the risk is one of damage to property. It is true that the duty may be seen as a contractual one, but in functional terms it will bite before any contract: e.g. a dry-cleaner asked to clean a fragile garment would probably be liable for failing to point out that the garment is likely be damaged by the treatment, and in effect the disclosure would have to be made at the pre-contract stage.

Lastly, within the traditional private law regime we deal with some cases of mistake under the rubric of unconscionable bargains. These cases are in one sense remarkable because in the classic examples the 'mistake' under which the claimant was labouring when he or she made the contract was merely one of the value of the property being sold—in *Fry v Lane*,[95] the value of the property that the sellers had just inherited and had agreed to sell for far less than its true value—yet the court allowed relief. We shall see that continental courts will usually exclude relief for mistake if the mistake is merely as to the value of the subject-matter of the contract.[96] But we have to note the stiff conditions that must be satisfied if a bargain is to be

---

[93] *Greaves & Co (Contractors) Ltd v Baynham Miekle & Partners* [1975] 1 WLR 1095.

[94] [1986] QB 644.

[95] (1888) 40 ChD 312.

[96] Below, pp 45 and 54.

held unconscionable. On the one side, the claimant must have been, in the words of the old cases, 'poor and ignorant'. There are various more modern formulations: in Megarry J's words, for 'poor and ignorant' now read 'member of the lower income group...[and] less highly educated'.[97] But even in the broad version of the doctrine applied in the Australian case of *Commercial Bank of Australia v Amadio*,[98] the claimant must be under some special disability. Simple ignorance of the facts does not seem to suffice. On the other side, the defendants must consciously have exploited the claimant's weakness. Lastly, the resulting contract must overall be oppressive to the claimant. There have been some suggestions recently that relief might be given more widely. In *Bank of Credit and Commerce International SA (In Liquidation) v Ali (No. 1)*[99] Lord Nicholls said that where the party to whom a general release was given knew that the other party has or might have a claim and knew that the other party was ignorant of this, to take the release without disclosing the existence of the claim or possible claim could be unacceptable sharp practice. The law would be defective if it did not provide a remedy, and while the case did not raise the issue, he had no doubt that the law would provide a remedy.[100] But nothing seems to have come of this as yet.

We need to look also beyond private law. First, we must consider 'regulatory regimes' in the narrow sense, especially in financial services. I suspect that many of us private lawyers have little idea of how far these now go. For example, investment business is largely regulated by the FSA by a combination of detailed Conduct of Business (COB) Rules

---

[97] *Cresswell v Potter* [1978] 1 WLR 255, 257, cited with apparent approval in *Credit Lyonnais Nederland NV v Burch* [1997] CLC 95, 101.

[98] (1983) 151 CLR 447 (H Ct).

[99] [2001] UKHL 8, [2002] 1 AC 251, at [32]–[33].

[100] Lord Bingham left the point open (at [20]); Lord Hoffmann thought that a person should not be allowed to rely upon a release in general terms if he knew that the other party had a claim and knew that the other party was not aware that he had a claim (at [70]).

and High Level Principles.[101] Some of the detailed rules
have been replaced by the Principles, but many rules
remain; and the Principles act as a supplement to the COB
rules, so that compliance with the rules is not enough if the
Principles are not complied with.[102] High Level Principle 6
requires firms to pay due regard to the interests of its
customers and to treat them fairly, and Principle 7 requires
them to pay due regard to the information needs of
clients and communicate information to clients in a way
which is clear, fair and not misleading. The effect is that
firms that are conducting regulated activities must both
make various disclosures and take steps to ascertain customers' needs and whether the product will be suitable for
those needs. These duties apply when the firms' own financial products are being sold and sometimes when it is other
firms' products that are being recommended.[103] Breach of
the rules has direct civil law consequences: it is actionable
as a breach of statutory duty.[104] What is required depends
on the client: the highest level applies to retail transactions
only but firms may have to make disclosure even to professional clients, whereas where the customer is (for example)
another investment firm, the duty is merely not to give
misleading information.[105]

Secondly, law reformers—and, I believe, comparative
law scholars—must also take into account the practices of
the profession or market, especially when these are sufficiently standardized to amount to something close to a
universal regime. In many situations there are standardized

---

[101] The FSA moved towards a more principles-based approach from
2005: R Fox (ed), *A Practitioner's Guide to the FSA Handbook* (5th edn, City
& Financial Publishing, Old Woking, 2005), 55.

[102] Ibid, 259, 263.

[103] Ibid, 311 *et seq*. There is an exemption for 'execution-only' transactions in 'non-complex financial instruments': ibid, 314.

[104] Financial Markets and Services Act 2000, s 150. However, the right
of action is limited to private persons (SI 2001/2256); and a breach of the
Principles is not actionable: *Regina (British Bankers Association) v Financial
Services Authority* [2011] EWHC 999 (Admin), [2011] Bus LR 1531.

[105] Fox (above, n 101), 279 *et seq*.

forms for pre-contract enquiries. When a business is sold, there are many precedents of enquiries aimed at revealing exactly what the buyer will be getting,[106] and these are often supplemented by various warranties which will be included in the contract of sale.[107] Equally, there are standard pre-contract enquiry forms for real property transactions.[108] For residential property, things have gone even further. The National Conveyancing Protocols[109] aim at speeding up the process.[110] Standard enquiry forms provided by the purchaser's solicitor have been replaced by lists of information about the property which the vendor's solicitor should prepare as soon as he or she is instructed—and they should try to get instructions as soon as the seller puts the property on the market, so that unnecessary delays in exchanging contracts can be avoided. There should also be savings if the property is offered to a succession of buyers: the system should avoid the vendor having to answer several slightly different sets of questions. So practice in effect requires the vendor to provide information on the most relevant questions; and if the vendor gives wrong or misleadingly incomplete information, the purchaser will have remedies for misrepresentation. There will also be a misrepresentation if vendors answer that they don't have information about something—say, whether the property is affected by a dispute with neighbours—when they know full well that it is.[111] In other words, standardized practices have developed to fill at least some

[106] e.g. LexisNexis, *BCLS Corporate Precedents*, Precedent 5, Due Diligence Questionnaire.

[107] e.g. ibid, Precedent 9, Business Sale Agreement, cl 14 and Sch 6.

[108] e.g. LexisNexis, *Encyclopedia of Forms and Precedents, Sale of Land* (vol 36), B 'Preliminary questions to be asked of seller' no 11, Preliminary enquiries: long form (freehold and leasehold).

[109] See Law Society Conveyancing Protocol (January 2011). For a period, sellers were required to provide Home Information packs but these have been discontinued: Home Information Pack (Suspension) Order 2010, SI 2010/1455, made pursuant to the Housing Act 2004, s 162.

[110] See K Gray and S Gray, *Elements of Land Law* (5th edn, OUP, Oxford, 2009), 8.1.11–8.1.13.

[111] *Walker v Boyle* [1982] 1 WLR 495.

of the gaps between what the law requires that the party be told and what a party needs to know in order to make an informed choice.

CONCLUSIONS

To assess the need for any change, we need to look not only at 'contract law' but also at regulation and practice. We find that in reality there are many exceptions to the basic rule that you have no duty to disclose facts that are adverse to the other party; indeed, in quite a number of cases you must go further and take active steps to enquire what the other party wants and thus, in effect, whether they know what it is they are buying. Even in areas in which there is no regulation requiring disclosure, standardized practices have been developed which will deal with most of the problems most of the time.

However, there are undoubtedly potential gaps in the system. First, there are some gaps in coverage. In the sale and supply of goods, the most obvious gap is where the sale or supply is not made in the course of a business, when the obligations to supply goods of satisfactory quality and that are fit for the buyer's particular purpose do not apply. Even when the sale or supply is in the course of a business, it is also possible that there are issues that fall outside the reach of the terms implied by the Sale of Goods Act. I wonder, for example, about customers who buy a 'new' car and are supplied with one which is undoubtedly new (in that it has not been driven for more than the normal delivery mileage) but which turns out to be a 'grey import', a car first registered in another country; or who were not told that the model they have ordered is about to be superseded by a new one. Either fact may have a major effect on the rate at which the car will depreciate in value, but I am not sure that either one is a matter of satisfactory quality or of fitness for the buyer's purpose.

With sales of land, *caveat emptor* remains firmly in place. There are no implied obligations, and thus no 'indirect' obligation to disclose, except in relation to defects of title.[112] Many points are covered by the questions in the protocol forms, but not all. There are no questions about matters such as the state of the wiring or of the drains on the property, even though the buyer may have little information about them—in my experience, these matters are not covered by the normal buyer's survey.

Secondly, the system probably works reasonably well for known unknowns, but there are also unknown unknowns. The more unusual the fact of which the buyer was ignorant, the less likely it is to be covered by either a specific duty or a question in the standard lists. Take the case of the couple who bought a house and then discovered that it had been the site of a horrific murder—and that parts of the victim's body had never been recovered and might still be secreted about the property.[113] The sellers were fully aware of this. On the facts, no blame can be attached to them; they had known nothing about the murder when they bought the house and, when they did find out, they were advised by their solicitor that neither the person who had sold it to them nor they themselves had any duty to disclose—as indeed the trial judge and the Court of Appeal held. Perhaps not surprisingly, the property information form does not ask the vendor to declare that no gruesome crime has been committed on the premises. I had assumed that this kind of problem would be dealt with by a general 'mop up' question. The enquiry form used in the murder case in fact included one but it was couched in subjective terms and in terms of the buyer's 'rights'—'is there any other information which *you* think the buyer may have a *right* to know?' On the facts the court had no difficulty in deciding that the sellers could properly have answered 'no'.[114] The question might have been redrafted in more objective terms, but in fact it has been dropped altogether.[115] So even when there

---

[112] See C Harpum (1992) 108 LQR 208; Treitel, para 9–129.
[113] *Sykes v Taylor-Rose* [2004] EWCA Civ 299, [2004] 2 P & CR 30.
[114] [2004] EWCA Civ 299 at [31] and [50].
[115] Seller's Property Information Form, 4th edition.

are standard enquiries, unknown unknowns may be a problem.

The Conveyancing Protocols are said to have been developed in response to a report by the Law Commission's Conveyancing Standing Committee in 1989.[116] This recommended that sellers should provide buyers with 'basic information'—information that would be important to any buyer—on a voluntary basis. In its consultation paper the Committee had provisionally proposed that sellers of property should have a duty to disclose all material facts about the property of which he was aware or ought to have been aware.[117] The Committee's Report rejected this approach on the basis that it would cause too much uncertainty, particularly as buyers may differ over whether a feature of a property is a disadvantage or not; and it might lead to buyers not making their own enquiries and, if they discovered a problem later, having to try to claim damages from the seller. It would be better to try to ensure that buyers were told the 'basic information' and were encouraged to ask about other matters that concerned them. No doubt the protocol scheme works very well in the vast majority of cases. We have to remember that most buyers will be professionally advised and those who do their own conveyancing will get plenty of warnings to be circumspect. However, there still seem to me to be potential loopholes—where the seller knows of some defect which would affect any normal buyer but which is not covered by the survey, or where the feature of the property is so unusual that it simply will not occur to the buyer to ask about it. The Committee does not discuss cases of this kind in its Report.

Thirdly, the *caveat emptor* approach depends on the buyer being sophisticated enough to ask the right questions—or to take advice. And the latter is not just a question of sophistication; it is also one of the cost of taking legal advice relative to the value of the deal.

---

[116] *Let the Buyer be well informed* (Law Commission, London, 1989); see Gray and Gray, above, n 110), 8.1.11.

[117] Caveat Emptor *in the Sale of Land* (Law Commission, London, 1988).

Lastly, I have a particular concern in cases like the German *Daktari* film rights case[118] which I referred to at the beginning of the chapter, where the parties have been in a commercial or social relationship for some time. Kötz describes the decision as dubious: 'tradesmen know full well where friendship stops and business begins'.[119] I am not so sure. With a complete stranger, you are likely to be circumspect and to make careful enquiries. If you know the other party and trust them, common sense tells us and empirical studies confirm that you are likely to be less concerned about ensuring that you have a legally water-tight agreement.[120] Equally, you may be much more ready to assume that the other party will tell you about adverse facts. Of course, there is already a duty of disclosure between partners and in situations in which we recognize that that there is a relationship of trust and confidence. Even though we now know that this requires something less than a full-blown fiduciary relationship, and even though the Court of Appeal has said that a relationship of trust and confidence may arise in relation to just a single transaction,[121] for a relationship of trust and confidence to arise outside the 'recognized' relationships like doctor and patient, we still seem to require the trusting party to make it absolutely clear to the other that they are positively look-ing to the other party to advise them. I don't think an English court would find a relationship of 'trust and confi-dence' in the English law sense on the facts of the *Daktari* case.

I end with the first case, *The Harriette N*.[122] We may not be worried about the outcome on the particular facts: it is

---

[118] BGH 31 January 1979, above, n 2.

[119] H Kötz, *European Contract Law* (Clarendon Press, Oxford, 1997), 200.

[120] See H Beale and A Dugdale, 'Contracts between Businessmen: Planning and the Use of Contractual Remedies' (1975) 2 British Journal of Law & Society 45, discussed further below, pp 112–114.

[121] *Turkey v Awadh* [2005] EWCA Civ 382, [2005] 2 FCR 7.

[122] *Statoil ASA v Louis Dreyfus Energy Services LP (The Harriette N)* [2008] EWHC 2257 (Comm), [2008] 2 Lloyd's Rep. 685; above, n 1.

arguable that a settlement contract is designed to achieve finality and each party should simply have to bear the risk of mistakes about the facts or about the law.[123] Moreover, what was at stake was a purely distributional question; whether or not the sellers were fully informed would not seriously affect their conduct in relation to anything else and would not lead to more efficient outcomes.[124] But those points were not the basis for the decision. The ground for decision—wholly in line with classical law—was simply that the mistake was only as to the surrounding facts and the other party had no obligation to point it out.

It seems to be fairly widely accepted that the blanket rule that one party can take knowing advantage of the other's ignorance is difficult to square with morality. In *Smith v Hughes* Cockburn CJ seemed to think that the buyer's silence about the mineral deposits might be immoral.[125] Later we will see that in some such cases, non-disclosure can be justified on the ground that it may lead to a general increase in welfare,[126] but when that is not the case, to keep silent and exploit the other's ignorance or mistake strikes me as morally wrong. In the next chapter we will see that in other legal systems, to take knowing advantage in this way is regarded as fraud.[127] I do not see the justification for a blanket rule of non-disclosure, unless it is either that we must give a very strong ideological message about self-reliance, or that we are unable to devise a workable rule to deal with the problem. So there is a case for continuing our investigation. Can we come up with a model that would go some way to rectifying these defects without becoming either hopelessly burdensome or uncertain? In the next

---

[123] Cf *Brennan v Bolt Burdon* [2004] EWCA Civ 1017, [2005] QB 303 (mistake of law). See Treitel, paras 8-024–8-025.

[124] See further below, pp 92–93.

[125] (1871) LR 6 QB 597, 604, quoted above, p 18. See further M Trebilcock, *The Limits of Freedom of Contract* (Harvard University Press, Cambridge Mass., 1993), 117–118.

[126] See below, pp 91–92.

[127] See below, pp 46 and 55.

chapter I will look at other systems to see how they approach the types of case that we have been discussing, before asking in Chapter 3 whether we can devise a workable model to replace the present law and, if so, whether we would wish to adopt it.

2

Mistake and Non-Disclosure in Other Systems

In cases in which C has entered the contract under a misapprehension as to the facts which is not shared by the other party D and which was not induced by D's statement or conduct, what do we find in other legal systems? What are the basic grounds for relief? What limits or controls, if any, are placed on relief for mistake? What values do the relevant systems appear to be prioritizing?

COMMONWEALTH LAWS

On this point the law in Ireland and in Scotland is the same as in England, and likewise in the common law systems of the Commonwealth countries or recent colonies that I have checked. Though on broader matters of mistake there are some divergences, with both the Australian[1] and Singaporean[2] courts seeing a larger role for equity than we allow in England, on the points we are considering the traditional approach seems to be maintained, together with the standard list of exceptions. This is the case in

---

[1] See *Taylor v Johnston* (1983) 151 CLR 522 (H Ct); Chitty, § 5–079 n 345.

[2] In *Chwee Kin Keong v Digilandmall.com Pte Ltd* [2005] 1 SLR 502, noted (2005) LQR 393 (and see Woan (2006) 22 JCL 81), *Great Peace Shipping Ltd v Tsavliris Salvage (International) Ltd (The Great Peace)* [2002] EWCA Civ 1407, [2003] QB 679 was not followed, and on the question of mistake as to terms (buyers trying to snap up an offer mistakenly placed on a website to sell laser printers at prices that were a fraction of the normal price), the court considered that, in addition to the common law rule, there is an equitable jurisdiction to set aside a contract for unilateral mistake in cases in which there is 'sharp practice' or 'unconscionable conduct' (at [76]–[77]). But there is no difference on unilateral mistake as to the facts.

Australia,[3] Brunei,[4] Hong Kong,[5] and India.[6] The Malaysian Contracts Act 1950 provides specifically that a contract is not voidable merely because it was caused by one of the parties to it being under a mistake as to a matter of fact.

In Australia, § 52 of the Federal Trade Practices Act 1974 (C'th) prohibited corporations from engaging, in trade or commerce, in conduct which is misleading or deceptive, or which is likely to mislead and deceive,[7] and provided the victim with a civil remedy for breach.[8] But though in the leading case[9] the High Court was at pains to stress that the meaning of the section does not depend on common law concepts such as duty,[10] the cases interpret 'conduct' in the traditional sense of requiring something more than mere silence unless there is a duty to speak. Black CJ said:

---

[3] J Carter, E Peden and G Tolhurst, *Contract Law in Australia* (5th edn, LexisNexis Butterworths, Chatswood NSW, 2007), para 18–14.

[4] s 23. Fraud (s 17) and misrepresentation (s 18) are defined in the conventional way. Exceptionally a guarantee obtained by concealment is invalid, s 96. On Singapore, Malaysia and Brunei see A Phang (ed), *Cheshire, Fifoot and Furmston's Law of Contract*, 2nd Singapore and Malaysian edition (Butterworths Asia, Singapore, 1998), ch 9.

[5] CP Chui, *Law of Contract in Hong Kong* (China and Hong Kong Law Studies, Hong Kong, 1988), paras 6.21 and 6.35. The law of mistake in Hong Kong is usefully discussed by Greenwood, 'Is Mistake Dead in Contract Law?' (2004) 34 Hong Kong LJ 495, but with no mention of a remedy for unilateral mistake as to the facts or non-disclosure.

[6] The Indian Contracts Act 1872, ss 17 and 18 define fraud and misrepresentation as requiring positive conduct on the part of the misrepresentor; the explanation to s 17 adds that mere silence does not amount to fraud unless there is a duty to speak. Section 20 provides for relief for mistake only where the mistake is common. See H Saharay (ed), *Dutt on Contract* (9th edn, Eastern Law House, Calcutta, 2000), 192, 199, 217 and 224.

[7] The Act was repealed by the Competition and Consumer Act 2010, with effect from 1 January 2011. Section 52 has been placed in the new Australian Consumer Law which is contained in Schedule 2 of the 2010 Act. Section 18(1) of the Australian Consumer Law now provides that '[a] person must not, in trade or commerce, engage in conduct that is misleading or deceptive or is likely to mislead or deceive.'

[8] Trade Practices Act 1974 s 52(1); see now the Australian Consumer Law, s 236 (damages) and s 237 (compensation orders).

[9] *Demagogue Pty Ltd v Ramensky* (1992) 110 ALR 608.

[10] Ibid, per Gummow J at 615–616.

Silence is to be assessed as a circumstance like any other. To say this is certainly not to impose any general duty of disclosure; the question is simply whether, having regard to all the relevant circumstances, there has been conduct that is misleading or deceptive or that is likely to mislead or deceive. To speak of 'mere silence' or of a duty of disclosure can divert attention from that primary question. Although 'mere silence' is a convenient way of describing some fact situations, there is in truth no such thing as 'mere silence' because the significance of silence always falls to be considered in the context in which it occurs. That context may or may not include facts giving rise to a reasonable expectation, in the circumstances of the case, that if particular matters exist they will be disclosed.[11]

The cases in which it was found that there had been a contravention all seem to be ones in which English lawyers would say there had been a misrepresentation, by provision of information that was misleadingly incomplete[12] or by conduct, for example by apparent readiness to grant a lease without revealing that a third person had a right of pre-emption.[13] In one case it was held that there was a breach of § 52 when a managing director did not reveal to his fellow directors his breach of fiduciary and statutory duties, but even there he was in breach of a duty under the articles of association.[14] Recently it was said in the High Court:

as a general proposition, s 52 does not require a party to commercial negotiations to volunteer information which will be of assistance to the decision-making of the other party.[15]

---

[11] *Demagogue Pty Ltd v Ramensky* (1992) 110 ALR 608 at 609–610.

[12] Ibid (vendor indicated that there would be access to site for development via driveway without revealing that the driveway was a public road and a licence would have to be obtained). See also *Winterton Constructions Pty Ltd v Hambros Australia Ltd* (1992) 111 ALR 649, 666.

[13] *Mikaelian v Commonwealth Scientific and Industrial Research Organisation* (1999) 163 ALR 172.

[14] *Groeneveld Australia Pty Ltd v Nolten* 2010 VSC 533 (unrep, 2010) at [66]–[67].

[15] *Miller & Associates Insurance Broking Pty Ltd v BMW Australia Finance Ltd* (2010) 270 ALR 204 (H Ct), per French CJ and Kiefel J at [22] (held that

The doctrine of unconscionability has been developed rather more in Australia than it has in England. In *Blomley v Ryan*,[16] Fullagar J said it requires the claimant to have been suffering from a 'special disadvantage', but added that this includes 'lack of assistance or explanation where assistance or explanation is necessary'. Obviously this might be applied to simple cases of mistake known to the other party, but it does not appear to have been. In his book, *Duress, Undue Influence and Unconscionable Dealing*, Enonchong cites cases where banks have been required to point out to uneducated customers that transactions are risky,[17] but he suggests that after *Crowe v Commonwealth Bank of Australia*[18] the courts are turning against this approach.[19] I see no suggestion that someone is disadvantaged within the meaning of the doctrine just because they were ignorant of or mistaken about some crucial fact.

Canada

I have found only two departures from this monolithic approach. The first is in Canada. There *Smith v Hughes* seems to be affirmed by modern cases,[20] and there is no recognition of anything like a general duty to disclose. Nor does the doctrine of unconscionability appear to have been used to deal with mistake cases.[21] However, there are two

---

if document about insurance policy not misleading, no breach by failing to point out that non-cancellable).

[16] (1956) 99 CLR 395, 402.

[17] e.g. *Elkofari v Permanent Trustee* [2002] NSWCA 413.

[18] [2005] NSWCA 41.

[19] N Enonchong, *Duress, Undue Influence and Unconscionable Dealing* (Sweet & Maxwell, London, 2006), para 26–025 *et seq*.

[20] S Waddams, *Law of Contract* (6th edn, Canada Law Book, Toronto, 2010) § 437. See *Radhakrishnan v University of Calgary Faculty Association* (2002) 215 DLR (4th) 624 (Alta CA) (no general duty to reveal facts when negotiating an ordinary contract: at [34]); *Ames v InvestoPlan Ltd* (1973) 35 DLR (3d) 613 (fraud requires active concealment: at 615); *Ryan v Moore* 2005 SCC 38, 254 DLR (4th) 1 at [76]–[77].

[21] See Waddams ch 14.

limited exceptions to the rule permitting non-disclosure. First, in cases in which a seller of a house knows that it is not fit for habitation, it has been held that the seller must disclose this fact.[22] Secondly, some courts have allowed relief when a contractor has submitted a bid based on a 'mistaken calculation'.

Earlier cases on mistakes in calculations, which have not been overruled, seem to take the orthodox position. In *Imperial Glass Ltd v Consolidated Supplies Ltd*[23] a contractor submitted a bid that was far too low because in calculating the square footage of glass required, an assistant had misplaced a decimal point. It was held that this did not prevent the employer from accepting the bid. In contrast, in *McMaster University v Wilchar Construction Ltd*[24] the contractor's bid had omitted a price escalation clause. The plaintiff knew that the contractor intended to include a clause and the court held that this was a mistake over the terms which prevented the plaintiff from accepting the contractor's offer.[25] However, in *Belle River Community Arena Inc v Kaufmann*[26] the *McMaster* case was treated as authority that a party cannot accept an offer 'which he knows has been made by mistake and which *affects* a fundamental term of the contract' (emphasis supplied)—a rather different and much broader proposition. It was also held that if the employer could not accept the bid because it knew of the mistake, there was no liability on the bid bond provided by the contractor: the effect of the bond was that the bonding company would be liable only if the contractor's bid was effectively accepted but the contractor refused to enter into a formal contract for the work.[27]

---

[22] See e.g. *McGrath v MacLean* (1975) 95 DLR (3d) 144; *Ward v Cudmore* (1987) 75 NBR (2d) 112 (QB).

[23] (1960), 22 DLR (2d) 759 (BC Court of Appeal).

[24] 22 DLR (3d) 9 (Ont SC).

[25] Ibid at [61]–[63]; the court applied *Hartog v Colin & Shields* [1939] 3 All ER 566.

[26] (1978) 87 DLR (3d) 761 (Ont SC), at [13].

[27] Ibid at [20].

In *R v Ron Engineering & Construction (Eastern) Ltd*[28] the contractor again submitted too low a bid because it had omitted an item from its calculations. Estey J, delivering the judgment of the Supreme Court of Canada, seemed determined that 'the integrity of the bidding system must be protected where under the law of contracts it is possible to do so'. He indicated not only that relief is confined to cases where 'the contractor did not intend to submit the tender in the form and substance it was' and the mistake is apparent on the face of the bid,[29] but that submission of the tender on terms that it could not be withdrawn without forfeiting a deposit was a separate contract ('contract A') from the contract to do the work itself ('contract B'). Only if the employer knew of the mistake at the time the tender was submitted would it be unable to enforce this separate contract. It is perhaps ironic that this two-contract analysis has become 'firmly ensconced'[30] as the basis on which a tenderer whose bid is improperly rejected may be given a remedy if the terms in which the tender was invited indicate that a conforming tender will be fairly considered.[31] When the tender was mistaken, lower courts have been astute to distinguish it by holding that 'contract A' never came into existence[32] or that, provided the contractor had not refused to go ahead by the time its bid was formally accepted, it could still be given relief from 'contract B'.[33] Appellate courts, however, have held that contract A is binding and the tenderer must enter contract B or pay

---

[28] (1981) 119 DLR (3d) 267.

[29] Ibid at [18]; see also at [22].

[30] G H L Fridman, QC, *The Law of Contract in Canada* (4th edn, Carswell, Scarborough Ont., 1999) (at p 42).

[31] See e.g. *MJB Enterprises Ltd v Defence Construction* (1951) Ltd 170 DLR (4th) 577 (SCC), noted in (1999) 115 LQR 583. See also J McCamus, 'Mistaken Bids and Unilateral Mistake: A new solution for an old problem' (2008) 87 Can Bar Rev 1, 6.

[32] e.g. *Toronto Transit Commission v Gottardo Construction Ltd* 68 OR (3d) 356 (mistake on face of document that was part of tender meant tender obviously did not conform).

[33] e.g. *Calgary (City) v. Northern Construction Co* (1982) 23 Alta LR (2d) 338 (QB).

damages.[34] But they have also said that a mistaken tenderer may be given relief in equity if the error was so disproportionate that to enforce the contract would be unconscionable.[35] Thus it seems that in Canada there may be relief when a tender is based on a wrong calculation, as well as when it states the price or terms themselves inaccurately, and the employer knows of the mistake before it accepts the tender, if it would be very unfair to enforce the mistaken bid.

I will come back to mistakes in calculations when I deal with parallel developments in the US.

New Zealand

In the Commonwealth the other major exception is New Zealand. The Contractual Mistakes Act 1977 allows relief when C entered the contract under a mistake that was not caused by a misrepresentation by the other party[36] if the existence of the mistake was known to D.[37] The court is given a very broad discretion to refuse to enforce the contract or, in effect, to adjust it.[38] Whether the mistake was about the terms or about the facts is immaterial.

It has been held that there is no mistake within the Act when the parties had not applied their minds to the question at all.[39] But though this is stated as if it applies to a

---

[34] *Calgary (City) v Northern Construction Co* [1986] 2 WWR 426 (Alta CA), 435; *Toronto Transit Commission v Gottardo Construction Ltd* (2005) 257 DLR (4th) 539.

[35] In the *Calgary* case at 436 and in the *Toronto Transit Commission* case at 547–8. See McCamus (above, n 31), who argues that this is a preferable basis for giving relief in such cases and when the mistake is as to the terms of the offer not the underlying calculation.

[36] Misrepresentation is dealt with by Contractual Remedies Act 1979 s 6. It is said it is 'not finally determined' whether s 6 also applies to a breach of any duty of disclosure: Burrows, Finn & Todd, *Law of Contract in New Zealand* (2nd edn, LexisNexis NZ, Wellington, 2002), 365.

[37] Section 6. See Appendix, below, p 130.

[38] Ibid, s 7.

[39] *New Zealand Refining Co Ltd v Attorney-General* (1992) 14 NZTC 9,006 (Greig J) and (1993) 15 NZTC 10,038 (CA); *Ladstone Holdings Ltd v Leonora Holdings Ltd* CP 308/SD00, [2006] 1 NZLR 211 (H Ct) at [70]–[87].

unilateral mistake by one party,[40] the cases involved are ones of common mistake; and it is hard to see that it will affect unilateral mistakes: even if C has not applied his mind to the matter, D (who must be actually aware of C's mistake) will have done.[41]

There are restrictions. The court may give relief only if

(i) D had actual knowledge of C's mistake;[42]
(ii) C did not bear the risk of mistake;[43] and
(iii) the mistake resulted in 'a substantially unequal exchange of values' or one party obtaining 'a benefit or obligation substantially disproportionate to the consideration therefor'.[44]

Further, s 4 provides:

(2) These powers ... are not to be exercised in such a way as to prejudice the general security of contractual relationships.

This is an interesting example of aspirational legislation. The court's discretion remains very wide.[45]

It would be useful to find out what policy concerns underlay the development of the various approaches, and to compare them to our own. The removal of the distinction between mistakes as to the terms and mistakes as to the facts from New Zealand law seems to have been little discussed at the time. The Report that preceded the legislation

---

[40] e.g. *Laws of New Zealand,* Contract (LexisNexis NZ Online), para 172; see also P Cooke in *NZ Refining* at 10.045.

[41] This may be why *Tri-star Customs & Forwarding Ltd v Denning* [1999] 1 NZLR 33, which involved a unilateral mistake, was said (at 38) to be possibly distinguishable on facts from *NZ Refining.*

[42] Constructive knowledge is not sufficient: *Tri-star Customs & Forwarding Ltd v Denning* [1999] 1 NZLR 33, 37; the position where the mistake is known but not its effect is open, *Vaucluse Holdings Ltd v NZ Guardian Trust Ltd* CA 237/99, 20 April 2000, Burrows et al (above, n 36) 298.

[43] Section 6(1)(c) (see Appendix, below, p 131).

[44] Section 6(1)(b)(i). For a recent case where the claim for relief for mistake failed because the exchange was not unequal, see *Janus Nominees Ltd v Fairhall* CA 336/2008, [2009] 3 NZLR 757.

[45] See further below, p 76.

stated merely that the *Smith v Hughes* distinction is 'illusory'. Coote wrote in 1988 that he was not convinced[46] but the issue was not raised in the review of the contract statutes published in 1993,[47] possibly because there had been no cases on the point by that date. I have found only one since. In *King v Williamson* V knew that P thought land being sold extended to a fence which was well beyond the true boundary, but did nothing to correct P's misapprehension.[48] Interestingly, Burrows et al still maintain that tacit acquiescence in another party's self-deception creates no legal liability, and treat *King v Williamson* as one of silence 'positively affirming' a misconception.[49]

But it has been pointed out that to ignore the distinction between a mistake as to the facts and one as to the terms is understandable given that the primary concern of draftsman and Act seems to have been to prevent unjust enrichment because the value of the parties' performances was very unequal. Section 6(1)(c) is key. If one is concerned with contractual justice in this sense, it doesn't make much sense to distinguish between bezoar stone offered on the misunderstanding that it is glass and a bezoar stone offered at a fraction of its value because of a slip on the price tag.[50] We will we return to this question of unjust enrichment later.[51]

---

[46] (1988) 13 NZULR 160, 167.

[47] New Zealand Law Commission, *Contracts Statutes Review* (Law Commission, Wellington, 1993).

[48] (1994) 2 NZ ConvC 95, 234. The facts seem similar to those of *Denny v Hancock* (1870) LR 6 Ch App 1, in which specific performance was refused but, unless the plan given to the buyer amounted to a positive misrepresentation (which it may well have done), the contract was presumably binding and damages could therefore be awarded against the purchaser who refused to go through with the sale: cf *Malins v Freeman* (1837) 2 Keen 25, 34–35; cf *Wood v Scarth* (1855) 2 K&J 33, 3 Eq Rep 385 (specific performance refused), (1858) 1 F&F 293 (damages awarded).

[49] Burrows et al (above, n 36) p 334.

[50] See discussion in D L Lange, 'Statutory Reform of the Law of Mistake' (1980) 18 Osgoode Hall LJ 428, 442–443.

[51] Below, p 77.

In Chapter 1 I pointed out that in some cases the so-called 'restatements' of European principles are not restatements of shared principles—they are only a statement of what the group thought to be generally acceptable, or even a simple compromise. So we should go behind the PECL and the DCFR to see what models are used in various national laws. In the space available I can deal only with French, German, and Dutch law, and with the Scandinavian laws.

At the risk of over-simplification, the various systems seem to adopt one of three broad approaches to mistake:

(1) to prioritize the protection of informed consent as an element of autonomy of the will, so that a party who was not fully informed about a vital matter may escape from the resulting agreement;

(2) to take a similar approach to autonomy of the will, but to balance against it the interest of the other party in the form of legitimate reliance on the contract; or

(3) to rely on general clauses that raise questions of both substantive and procedural fairness or even the purely substantive question, whether the resulting exchange was equal.

France

French law seems in broad terms to represent the first approach. It seems to be the readiest to give relief on the ground that one party was not fully informed and therefore did not genuinely consent.

Given that the *Code civil* was adopted in 1804, it is not surprising that it is the closest to Roman Law, which took the approach that a consensual contract required subjective agreement and that if one party was mistaken as to an essential element—the price, the person he was contracting with, or the substance of the subject-matter, as when I buy something which I think is made of gold but which in fact is brass—there is simply no contract because I have not consented,[52] and essentially subjective agreement was required for a valid contract.[53]

Under Article 1110(1) of the French *Code civil*:

Error is a cause of nullity of an agreement... when it goes to the very substance of the object of the agreement.

The contract affected by error is not absolutely null: it is a case of relative nullity in which annulment may be declared at the instance of the mistaken party.[54]

While many of the cases in which the contract is annulled under this article are ones in which relief would also be given in English law because C's mistake resulted from being given incorrect information by D,[55] or because they are cases of common mistake, the French courts can declare the contract annulled where the mistaken party would certainly get no relief under English law. Perhaps the best-known example is the *Poussin* case,[56] where the claimants had sold a picture which they understood could not possibly be by Nicholas Poussin, despite the family tradition that it was by him; they had been advised that it was probably by an artist of the school of Carracci. The Louvre used its right of pre-emption to buy the painting without revealing their view that it was almost certainly a Poussin, and they later displayed it as such. After protracted litigation, the

---

[52] See Nicholas, 84–85; Zimmermann, *Obligations*, 587 *et seq.*

[53] Zimmermann, *Obligations*, 564.

[54] Avoidance is not by notice to the other party but by declaration of the court in response to an *action en nullité*: art 1117 CC; Nicholas, 77–78. Cartwright, 'Defects of Consent in Contract Law', in A Hartkamp et al (eds), *Towards a European Civil Code* (4th edn, Kluwer, Alphen aan den Rijn, 2011), 537, 547. Invalidity may also be raised as a defence to an action to enforce the contract: Malaurie no 700.

[55] e.g. Cass civ 23 November 1931, DP1932.1.129, ann Josserand; Gaz Pal 1932.1.96 (trans Ius Commune casebook no 10.25).

[56] Or rather the series of cases: the final stages were Cass civ 13 December 1983, JCP 1984.II.20186 and Cour d'appel, Versailles, 7 January 1987 (trans Ius Commune casebook no 10.26).

contract was annulled on the basis that the sellers' mistake was as to the subject-matter (rather than, for instance, merely the value of the picture) because they thought it definitely was not a Poussin when in fact it might well be.

French law is wider than the Roman law of mistake not only because it has abandoned the Roman categories but also because it extends more clearly beyond what can be called the substance of the subject-matter. Pothier argued that it sufficed that the mistake was as to the qualities of the subject-matter that parties had in view when they made the contract.[57] In practice many cases involve a mistake as to some essential characteristic that is mainly important to one of the parties, such as whether the land being bought is suitable for the development that the buyer has in mind. In these 'constructability' cases[58] it seems that what matters is whether the importance to C was known to D, or perhaps accepted by D—the exact requirement has been a matter of some discussion.[59]

In addition, it is traditionally said that there will be no relief for a mere error of motive.[60] A traditional example is the father who buys a wedding dress for his daughter[61] (having a daughter as yet unmarried, I would prefer to update the example to a young woman who buys a wedding dress for herself), in ignorance of the fact that her fiancé has just married someone else and will therefore be unavailable at least for a frustratingly long period. Given the extended notion of substance which has been accepted, it is not always easy to distinguish a mistake of substance from mere mistake in motive; for example, in the 'constructability' cases the buyer's motive is to develop the land and the outcomes cases do not seem to depend on whether it matters to the seller that the development is possible (e.g. because he is retaining adjoining land which would benefit

---

[57] See Nicholas, 85.
[58] See Nicholas, 86; examples are given in Terré no 216 n 5.
[59] See Nicholas, 92–93.
[60] e.g. Terré no 220.
[61] e.g. Kramer, IECL § 29.

from it). The distinction seems to be that there will be no error of substance unless the mistake relates in some way to the nature of the thing, rather than what it may be used for,[62] or the purpose is an agreed part of the contract.[63]

It is interesting to note the way these two issues are resolved in the *Avant-projet Catala*, one of the purposes of which was to bring the *Code civil* into line with the jurisprudence.[64] If the mistake was to the substance of the subject-matter, it is sufficient that the non-mistaken party knows of its importance to the mistaken party.[65] An error as to motive may also be a ground for annulment, but only if the parties have expressly made it a decisive element of their consent.[66] The draft produced by the Ministry of Justice is almost identical on this point.[67] The constructability cases would come under the first provision, while the second would preclude relief in the wedding dress case, unless the wedding or the continuing existence of the engagement were made an express condition of the contract.

Having set the basis for a wide doctrine, however, the courts have imposed a number of limits. First, a mistake which is merely as to the value is not a ground of nullity.[68] Secondly, a party may not have the contract annulled if its mistake was 'inexcusable'.[69] Thirdly, there will be no relief for mistake if the party accepted the risk—which may be express or, it seems, by implication from the circumstances.[70]

---

[62] Nicholas, 92.

[63] See Malaurie no 505, n 30.

[64] P Catala, 'Présentation générale de l'avant-projet', para 5; Ius Commune casebook, 79.

[65] *Avant-projet Catala*, art 1112–1.

[66] Ibid, art 1112–5.

[67] Ministry draft of May 2009 (see above, p 12, n 51), arts 47 and 49.

[68] Malaurie no 505; Terré no 220.

[69] Malaurie no 506; Terré no 223. The cases cited in both books seem to involve fairly extreme carelessness on the part of the mistaken party. Terré states that the law will not protect a party who has the necessary information or who could obtain it easily.

[70] As when the attribution of a picture was known to be in doubt: Cass 1 civ, 24 March 1987, D. 1987.488; see Terré no 217, text at n 5; *Avant-projet Catala* art 1112–1(3).

Thus relief for mistake as to the substance is given relatively freely in French law. The normal remedy is avoidance.[71] Commentators suggest that if the party who has avoided the contract was mistaken through his own fault, he might be made liable in damages for any loss he has caused the other party.[72] This is the position taken by doctrine, but in practice it seems that this sanction is not demanded. Instead the normal sanction is to refuse annulation for error.[73]

The English cases we considered in Chapter 1 were all ones in which C's mistake was known to D. It should be noted that this is not a necessary element of mistake in French law. Provided that D was aware of the importance of the subject-matter, it is not necessary that he or she was aware of C's mistake or ignorance of the crucial fact.

Indeed, if the non-mistaken party was aware of the mistake, the case is likely to be treated as one not just of mistake but of fraud. Originally, French law like English law required active misconduct, but the courts have long recognized that the *manoeuvres* required by article 1116 can include *dol par réticence*, deliberate silence which is intended to mislead the other party. The classic example is the *Pig Farm* case.[74] The claimants bought a country house from the defendant who failed to reveal that a farm for 400 pigs was about to be set up 100m from the house. The purchasers were allowed to recover the 10,000 FF they had paid on account:

[71] If the mistaken party does not wish to avoid the contract he may recover damages if there was fault on the part of the non-mistaken party (or his agent): Cass civ, 29 November 1968, Gaz Pal 1969. II.63. 'This is not a question of error as to the substance but one of responsibility': Malaurie (3rd edn, 2007), no 501. The basis of liability is considered to be the same as that for pre-contractual fault: see Nicholas, 110.

[72] Terré no 227, but no examples are given. Cf § 122 BGB.

[73] See J Ghestin, *La Formation du contrat* (3rd edn, Paris: LGDJ, 1993), para 522.

[74] Cass civ 3, 2 October 1974, Bull civ III.330; D1974, IR.252; RGLJ 1975.569, ann Blanc (trans Ius Commune casebook no 10.41).

[D]eceit may consist and take the form of silence on the part of a contracting party who conceals from the other party a fact which, had it been known by the other party, would have caused him not to enter the contract.

If the case is one of fraud, the mistaken party may again have the contract annulled, and may claim damages. Importantly, the limitations imposed in cases of mistake do not apply.[75] Thus it does not matter that the resulting error is not as to substantial quality of thing sold,[76] but is merely to a matter of motive. So the young woman can get out of the contract if the dressmaker knows the wedding cannot take place, for example because it is the dressmaker herself who has married the fiancé. Even a mistake as to value may suffice if it was induced by fraud.

Just as in England, proof of fraud is difficult, and when the alleged fraud is by silence the difficult thing to prove will be the intention to deceive. But as Nicholas put it,[77] the requirement has been side-stepped by a second development.

This is that the courts have accepted academic arguments that there is sometimes a positive duty to give information. So where a buyer of land from a professional seller discovered that he would never be able to get planning permission to build on the land, the sale was annulled. The seller objected that it had not intentionally deceived the buyer but the Cour de cassation affirmed the lower court, remarking that the seller had a duty to inform.[78]

The development is well-documented, for example by Ghestin,[79] by Nicholas,[80] and by Legrand,[81] where it

---

[75] Compare art 1116 CC (fraud) to art 1110 (mistake) and see Malaurie no 511, 512.

[76] Ibid.

[77] Nicholas, 103.

[78] Cass Civ. 3.2.1981, D. 1984.J.497; see Nicholas, 103.

[79] See J Ghestin, 'The pre-contractual Obligation to Disclose Information: French Report', in D Harris and D Tallon (eds), *Contract Law Today: Anglo-French Comparisons* (Clarendon Press, Oxford, 1989), 151.

[80] Nicholas, 102 *et seq*.

[81] P Legrand, 'Pre-contractual Disclosure and Information: English and French law compared' (1986) 6 OJLS 322.

is explained how it was constructed out of a number of elements—error, *dol par réticence*, and by arguing by analogy to the Code provisions on liability for hidden defects in property sold and other legislative provisions—a process termed 'amplifying induction'. The *Avant-projet Catala* may be taken as an up-to-date summary of the position (I quote the translation by Cartwright and Whittaker[82]):

Art 1110

If one of the parties knows or ought to have known information which he knows is of decisive importance for the other, he has an obligation to inform him of it.

However, this obligation to inform exists only in favour of a person who was not in a position to inform himself, or who could legitimately have relied on the other contracting party, by reason (in particular) of the nature of the contract or the relative positions of the parties.

...

Art 1110–1

In the absence of an intention to deceive, a failure to fulfil an obligation to inform gives rise to liability in the party subject to it.

Given the wide relief that French law already gave in cases of both mistake and fraud, it is hard to know how far the development of this *obligation de renseignement* is in fact a change of substance rather than one of form. It may seem to be mainly recasting the matter in terms of a positive duty to give information rather than in terms of when someone who is ill-informed may have relief.[83] But it certainly will enable a party who has entered a contract under a misapprehension which is not sufficiently serious to justify avoidance on the ground of mistake, and who cannot prove fraud, to recover damages nonetheless.

French authors identify a number of differing policies or philosophies underlying the law of contract. It is evident

---

[82] In J Cartwright, S Vogenauer and S Whittaker (eds), *Reforming the French Law of Obligations: Comparative Observations on the Avant-projet de réforme du droit des obligations et de la prescription* (Hart, Oxford, 2009), 639.

[83] Sefton-Green, 10–11 points out that whereas relief for mistake is based on protecting the mistaken party and fraud on sanctioning the fraudulent party, the duty to disclose seems to straddle the two.

that French law still has a strong attachment to notions of voluntarism and the autonomy of the individual. While, as Rouhette argued, the *Code civil* does not provide simply that what was willed should be enforced, but mediates it through a variety of legal requirements,[84] French lawyers still seem in general to take the view that a party's expression of will should not be binding if the party's consent was not correctly informed. But notions of contractual solidarity have also had a powerful influence. These are not just notions that a party should take some account of the interests of the other party. Demogue put forward the idea that a contract was not the result of tensions between antagonistic interests but 'a little society in which each must work towards a common end which is the sum of the individual ends pursued by the parties'.[85] It may also involve the idea that, as Ripert put it in 1948, individual rights are given to man for him to fulfil his social function.[86] Therefore contractual situations must be controlled and modified so that they conform to the general interest (and we can be sure that those who espoused this view were not taking the same view of what is good for society as, say, Chicago economists). Ripert was writing against a background of extensive controls over contracts—of employment, for food and for housing, and that interpretation of solidarity is probably no longer defended. Jamin has put forward a 'new' interpretation of solidarity.[87] He looks particularly at cases involving networks of contracts—dealerships and distribution contracts, in which the courts have restrained the firm that controls the network from acting without

[84] G Rouhette, 'The Binding Nature of Contractual Obligations: The Obligatory Force of Contract in French Law' in Harris and Tallon (above n 79), 38.

[85] R Demogue, *Traité des obligations en general*, t 6, (Rousseau, Paris, 1931), no 3; see Terré no 41.

[86] G Ripert, *Le Régime démocratique et le droit civil moderne* (2nd edn, LGDJ, Paris, 1948), 251.

[87] C Jamin, 'Plaidoyer pour le solidarisme contractual', in *Le contrat au debut du XXIeme siècle: Études offerts à Jacques Ghestin* (LGDJ, Paris, 2001), 441.

paying reasonable regard to the interests of the network member. Jamin argues that solidarity now requires that the classical presumption that the parties are equal should be replaced by one that they are unequal. French views are certainly not monolithic, however. Carbonnier's response to Demogue was that it is astonishing that, in an age when marriage might perhaps be transformed into a contract, some people dream of turning a contract into a marriage.[88] Terré, Simler, and Lequette claim that Demogue, in arguing that contracts should be treated like partnerships, was seeking to assimilate 'exchange contracts' and 'organization contracts', which are different and incompatible notions; and they are fiercely critical of notions of contractual solidarity in general and of Jamin in particular, arguing that his approach will leave too much to judicial discretion.[89] But French legal thinking still seems strongly influenced by solidarity, and it is often remarked that it has much stronger moral overtones than the law this side of the Channel.[90] These persist into the recent proposals—Dominique Fenouillet has written that proposals in the draft reforms suggested by the French Ministry of Justice, 'reflect moral considerations more than economic ones'.[91]

Given this intense debate, it may seem surprising that there seems to be little specific discussion of the policy underlying the (to English eyes) very liberal French rules on mistake and non-disclosure. One of the first writers on the duty of disclosure, Juglart, based it firmly on solidarity.[92] One might have expected fierce attacks from those who oppose notions of solidarity entering contract law. Possibly the answer is that to a French lawyer, thinking of contractual freedom as linked to individual autonomy, there is not the same conflict as over some other topics. In many of the cases we are considering, notions of

---

[88] Carbonnier, *Les obligations*, t 4, no 113, quoted in Terré no 41.
[89] Terré, no 42.
[90] e.g. Harris and Tallon (above, n 79), 'Conclusions', 385.
[91] D Fenouillet [2009] 1 RDC 279, 280.
[92] M de Juglart, 'L'Obligation de renseignements dans les contrats' (1945) Rev tr DC 1.

autonomy and notions of solidarity seem to point in the same direction: seeking to ensure that the contracting party is adequately informed, and allowing escape if he or she was not.

Some French authors at least have expressed some concern at the readiness with which the relief for mistake seems to be granted. For example, some years ago Fabre-Magnan argued that mistake should not apply to (and there would be no duty of disclosure of) a matter that went to the mistaken party's own *prestation*, what they had to deliver or do—so that the sellers in the *Poussin* case would have no relief because their mistake was as to the nature of the picture they had undertaken to deliver.[93] This suggestion does not seem to have been accepted, however; it is expressly rejected in the *Avant-projet Catala.*[94]

Recently there has been some retrenchment. Thus the Cour de cassation has more than once held that there is no duty to point out a mistake as to value even when the other party is in a weak position, though it left open the possibility that there might be *dol par réticence* in such a case.[95] But French law still goes far in allowing a party to escape the contract on the ground that it was not fully informed and in trying to prevent misinformed decisions from occurring, and I have not found many criticisms of this approach. A commentator on the PECL carefully explained their more restrictive approach, limiting relief to cases in which the mistake was or should have been known to the other party, but rejected it outright as failing to provide adequate

---

[93] M Fabre-Magnan, 'Duties of Disclosure and French Contract law' in J Beatson and D Friedmann (eds), *Good Faith and Fault in Contract Law* (Clarendon Press, Oxford, 1995), 99.

[94] *Avant-projet Catala*, art 1112–1(2); see likewise Ministry draft of May 2009 art 47.

[95] Civ 3e, 17 January 2007, D, 2007, 1051, note D Mazeaud, et 1054, note Ph Stoffel-Munck; RTD civ, 2007, 335, obs J Mestre et B Fages; Defrénois 2007, 443, obs E Savaux; RDC 2007/3, 703, obs Y M Laithier; JCP 2007, éd. G, II, 10042, note Ch Jamin; Cont conc conso 2007, n° 117, obs L Leveneur.

protection for autonomy of the will.[96] We have seen that both the Catala and the Ministry drafts have followed a traditional line on this point.

Germany

The approach of the Bürgerliches Gesetzbuch (BGB), Germany's civil code, to mistake might have been completely different to that of the French *Code civil*, and in some respects it is indeed different. The drafters were heavily influenced by the will theory advocated by Savigny.[97] Savigny saw the binding nature of the contract being based on the declared will of the parties, and considered that if the declaration did not match their actual will, it should not bind.[98] But he drew a distinction between the declaration and the motivation for the declaration, and considered that in principle a mistake that affected only the motivation, rather than the declaration, should be irrelevant. The first draft of the BGB applied this very literally, and gave relief only for errors in declaration, which would render the declaration of no effect.[99] The First Commission

---

[96] G Loiseau, 'La qualité du consentement', in P Rémy-Corlay and D Fenouillet, *Les concepts contractuels français à l'heure des PDEC* (Dalloz, Paris, 2003) 65, 73.

[97] K Zweigert and H Kötz, *An Introduction to Comparative Law* (3rd edn, trans T Weir, Clarendon Press, Oxford, 1998) 413; Markesinis 277–278; Zimmermann, *Obligations* 614–617 (Markesinis, 278 refers also to Windscheid, *Lehrbuch des Pandektenrechts* I (6th edn, Rütten & Loening, Frankfurt, 1887), § 78, 233 *et seq*); Kramer, IECL § 24.

[98] The BGB did not follow Savigny in treating the declaration as void: an operative mistake renders the contract voidable under §142 BGB. Avoidance is by notice to the other party, § 143, which must be given without culpable delay after the ground for avoidance is known, with a maximum period of 10 years from the date of the contract: § 121(1). On time limits and the effects of avoidance see Markesinis, 278.

[99] Section 119(1) provides:

(1) A person who, when making a declaration of intention, is in error as to its content, or did not intend to make a declaration of such content at all, may avoid the declaration if it may be assumed that he would not have made it with knowledge of the facts and with reasonable appreciation of the situation.

charged with drafting the BGB also thought that error in motivation should not be relevant; the mistaken party is adequately protected by other remedies, principally for breach of contract.[100] However, Savigny had recognized that it would be hard to reconcile this sharp distinction between declaration and motivation with the Roman doctrine of *error in substantia*,[101] which he had re-interpreted in a broad fashion to include errors about the 'commercial category' into which the item should fall.[102] The final draft of the BGB was more generous: § 119 II provides that

(2) An error as to those characteristics of a person or thing which are regarded in business as essential is regarded in the same way as an error as to the content of a declaration.[103]

The second drafting Commission justified this partly by 'the needs of business', though they seem to have had some doubts about what mistakes should fall within the provision: they added that it would be better to leave the definition to legal science and practice than to attempt to legislate.[104]

So in German law too there is potential for relief when a party enters a contract because of a mistake about the

---

This applies to both the case where the party uses a word mistakenly thinking it has one meaning when it has another (*Inhaltsirrtum*) and 'slips of the pen', when the party intends one thing but writes another (*Erklärungsirrtum*). It seems that the courts sometimes interpret *Inhaltsirrtum* broadly to cover situations that look more like a mistake about the facts: see the examples given in Zweigert & Kötz (above, n 97), 414. It has also been used to cover some cases in which a party is mistaken about the legal effect of the contract: Markesinis, 296.

[100] Motive, vol 1, p 199, cited Markesinis, 297. See the account in Zimmermann, *Obligations*, 616. E Zitelmann, *Irrtum und Rechtsgeschäft* (Duncker & Humblot, Leipzig, 1879) had taken a similar view: Zimmermann, *Obligations*, 617.

[101] Markesinis, 278.

[102] Zimmermann, *Obligations*, 617.

[103] A distinguished German scholar has remarked that 'the phrasing sounds embarrassed, since these mistakes of fact...are dealt with by way of a legal fiction': Kramer, IECL, § 24.

[104] Protokolle der zweiten Kommission para 235, quoted in B Mugdan 'Die gesamten Materialien zum Bürgerlichen Gesetzbuch fuer das deutsche Reich: Band I – Einführungsgesetz und Allgemeiner Teil' (1979) Scientia Verlag Alen 718.

characteristics of the subject-matter. But again there are limits. One is imposed by § 119(2) BGB itself: the error must be to a characteristic 'regarded in business as essential'. This is an objective criterion and it said that the German courts have used it to prevent the section causing 'major distortions in German Law'.[105] A mistake which is not about the subject-matter or is not regarded as important in an objective sense is classified as one of motive only and there is no relief.[106] Other limits are imposed by the courts. The effect of minor mistakes is limited by a causal requirement: not only must the mistake have caused the party to enter the contract, but there will not be an adequate causal link unless it would have been reasonable for the mistaken party, had he known the truth, not to enter into it.[107] The price is not treated as an essential quality of the thing within § 119(2) BGB, so again errors as to value are not a ground for relief.[108] There is a further limitation which is not found in French law. This is that the article does not apply where the BGB's rules on defects in goods apply. This obviously prevents sellers who unknowingly delivered goods that are defective for escaping liability on the ground of mistake,[109] but also it prevents a buyer from using § 119 where it would produce a more favourable result.[110]

---

[105] Markesinis, 298.

[106] For an example of a mistake that was only of motive, see BGH 28 February 2002, BGH NJW 2002, 2312 (trans Markesinis case no 87) (whether party's earnings under contract affected by VAT).

[107] Markesinis, 293.

[108] Markesinis, 298. Likewise, the practical usefulness of goods sold for a particular purpose will only be one the goods' essential characteristics if that was recognizably the basis on which the complaining party entered the contract: see BHG 18 December 1954, BGHZ 16,54, Ius Commune casebook case no 10.18 and following notes. Equally, German law faces the same distinction as is found in English law between mistakes in an offer and mistakes in the 'calculations' that precede the offer: compare above p 39 and below p 69. This distinction is criticized as unrealistic: Markesinis 283, 295; Kramer, IECL § 80.

[109] See the discussion in BGH 8 June 1988, BGH NJW 1988, 2597 (trans Markesinis case no 89).

[110] See Markesinis, 314.

Nonetheless, the potential for relief is broad: the mistake may be unilateral and there is no requirement that the fact of the mistake be known to the other party.[111] Moreover, the fact that the mistaken party was careless is immaterial. (The first draft of the BGB contained a bar for gross negligence but this was rejected by the final Commission.[112])

But at the same time the final Commission imposed a rule that distinguishes the German position: they provided for the protection of the other party's reliance where that reliance was justified.[113] § 122 provides that the C who avoids the contract must compensate the D for its reliance loss unless D 'knew the ground of the nullity or rescission or did not know of it due to negligence'. It is said that a typical claim for reliance loss under this section will be a claim for a lost opportunity to buy or sell the goods elsewhere.[114]

Clearly, where it applies, § 122 provides a strong disincentive to avoidance if the other party has already relied on the contract. It must be noted however that it does not apply if the other party knew, or should have known, that there was a mistake.[115]

German law also recognizes that if D knew of C's mistake and deliberately kept silent, D may be treated as fraudulent; and again relief is given for fraud more freely than for mistake.[116] But here there is a qualification: there is fraud by silence only if D had a duty to disclose the information that C did not have.[117] The process in Germany seems to

---

[111] Such a requirement was explicitly rejected by the Commission: Markesinis, 278. Thus the German doctrine of mistake is sometimes described as 'psychological': see the sources cited by Markesinis, 283.

[112] Munch K. BGB s 119, Rn 53.

[113] Zimmermann, *Obligations*, 612 attributes this idea to Grotius.

[114] Markesinis, 289.

[115] § 122 BGB is often referred to as an emanation of the doctrine of *culpa in contrahendo*, e.g Markesinis, 279; but compare Zimmermann, *Obligations*, 602 and 614, who points out that liability is not based on fault.

[116] Compare §123 BGB (fraud and § 119(2) and see e.g. RGZ 81, 13; see also H Kötz, *European Contract Law* (trans T Weir, Clarendon Press, Oxford, 1997), 196.

[117] Markesinis, 305.

have been the reverse of the French: rather than a duty to disclose being built on *dol par réticence*, liability for fraud by silence in German law seems to have been built on the duty to disclose.[118] The duty to disclose was derived from the notion of *culpa in contrahendo*, fault in the contracting process. *Culpa in contrahendo* was developed by von Jhering[119] for cases where one party was unaware that the contract which had been made was unenforceable for formal reasons. There were some reflections of the idea in the original BGB.[120] The courts developed and expanded *culpa in contrahendo* to cover other forms of fault in the contracting process, such as negligent injury to a prospective customer,[121] carelessly misleading the other as to your intentions,[122] breaking off negotiations,[123] carelessly giving wrong information, and the failure to disclose. At least in the last two categories, the courts have developed the doctrine partly on the basis of § 242 BGB[124] (the famous section which requires contracts to be performed in good faith).[125] *Culpa in contrahendo* is now incorporated into the BGB.[126]

---

[118] See K Zweigert & H Kötz (above, n 97), 425.

[119] R. von Jhering, 'Culpa in contrahendo oder Schadensersatz bei nichtigen oder nicht zur Perfection gelangten Verträgen', *Jahrbücher für die Dogmatik des heutigen römischen und deutschen Privatrechts*, 1861.IV.1.

[120] Markesinis, 94 (e.g. former § 307, liability of party who entered a contract that he (but not the other party) should have known to be impossible; and perhaps § 122, but see above, n 115).

[121] RG 7 December 1911, RGZ 78, 239 (trans Ius Commune casebook case no 3.15). An action in tort was not possible because the fault was that of an employee and German law lacks a general notion of vicarious liability: See W van Gerven, J Lever and P Larouche, *Cases, materials and text on Tort Law* (Hart, Oxford, 2000), 480 *et seq*.

[122] RG 5 April 1922, RGZ 104, 265 (trans Markesinis case no 12) (party liable if gave appearance of wishing to buy when in fact intended to sell).

[123] e.g. BGH 10 July 1970, LM § 276 [Fa] BGB No. 34, NJW 1970.1840, trans Beale case no 9.14 (though in that case the claim failed). See generally J Cartwright and M Hesselink, *Precontractual Liability in European Private Law* (CUP, Cambridge, 2008); Ius Commune casebook, ch 9.

[124] § 242 *Performance in accordance with the principle of good faith*

The debtor must perform his obligation in accordance with the requirements of good faith, taking into account the prevailing practice.

[125] Markesinis, 305 and see the *Daktari* case, above p 1, n 2, para 3.

[126] § 241(2) ('An obligation may also, depending on its contents, oblige each party to take account of the rights, legal interests and other interests

It is said that the courts found a need to develop liability for misleading the other party on the basis of *culpa in contrahendo*,[127] and looking at the structure of the relevant articles of the BGB it is clear why. Without it there would be no remedy for cases of non-fraudulent misrepresentation[128] that did not give rise to a mistake within § 119(2) (for example, because it did not involve 'a quality considered essential in business'), nor (given the restrictive nature of the German provisions on liability in tort for non-physical losses[129]) could damages be awarded for 'negligent misrepresentation'. But even if it was aimed primarily at cases of positive misrepresentation,[130] it was formulated as a duty to inform. Where, then, there is a duty to disclose, the ill-informed party may recover damages for non-disclosure of a fact which does not go to the substance and, if they would not have entered the contract, even rescission may be permitted if this is the best way of restoring them to the status quo ante.[131] Where the non-disclosure was dishonest (it seems the requirements are broadly similar to those of *Derry v Peek*[132]), there will be fraud by silence and therefore, as in France, the more generous rules governing avoidance for fraud will apply.

It is difficult to state when the duty to disclose will apply because the decisions are 'fact-specific'.[133] Examples include sellers of vehicles who fail to reveal that the

of the other party') and § 311(2) ('An obligation with duties under section 241(2) also comes into existence by (1) the commencement of contract negotiations...').

[127] Markesinis, 303.

[128] And fraud is narrowly defined: see Markesinis, 311.

[129] See Markesinis and Unberath, *The German Law of Torts* (4th edn, Hart, Oxford, 2002), 52 *et seq.*

[130] An example that is available in English is BGH 25 May 1977, BGHZ 69, 53 (trans Markesinis case no 93).

[131] Markesinis, 311 citing BGB NJW 1985, 1769; NJW 1993, 2107.

[132] (1889) 14 App Cas 337. Thus a reckless statement will amount to deceit: Markesinis, 305. However, in English law a dishonest motive is not needed, whereas in German law a party is not fraudulent if they did not recognize that the matter might be important to the other: Markesinis, 311.

[133] Markesinis, 307 and 308.

vehicle has been damaged in an accident[134] (where the problem seems to have been that although the damage had been repaired, some effects of the accident might not appear until a long time afterwards; if the vehicle had a defect within the sales provisions, e.g. § 434 BGB, the buyer would only have a remedy for breach of contract and not one for *culpa in contrahendo*[135]); sellers of land who fail to reveal defects such as damp or contamination;[136] 'constructability' cases;[137] and cases in which the seller of a business had not revealed falls in profitability after the period for which accounts had been provided.[138]

Markesinis et al identify two criteria:

(1) the overwhelming importance of the information to the ill-informed party; and

(2) the existence of a relationship of trust between the parties, the prime example being the *Daktari* film rights case.[139]

Some cases involving non-disclosure by car dealers are also put into the second category.[140] If the public attitude towards car dealers is the same in Germany as it is in England, 'trust' in a dealer seems fictitious; Kötz suggests that the cases are really to be explained by a third criterion: the seller is in a much better position to discover the defect than the buyer.[141]

Just how far the cases on disclosure go beyond what would happen in English law it is hard to say. Many

---

[134] e.g. BGH 3 March 1982, NJW 1982, 1386, trans Ius Commune casebook no 10.43 (DE).

[135] Markesinis, 314.

[136] Markesinis, 308 referring to BGH NJW 1993, 1703 and BGH NJW 1995, 1549.

[137] Markesinis, 308 referring to BGH NJW 2003, 2381 and BGH NJW-RR 1988, 394.

[138] e.g. BGH NJW 2001, 2163; BGH 6 December 1996, BGH NJW-RR 1996, 429 (trans Markesinis case no 91).

[139] See above, pp 1–2 and 29.

[140] Markesinis, 309.

[141] H Kötz, (above, n 116), 201.

of the cases are of 'misrepresentation by half-truth'[142] or where the facts have changed between the time the statement was made and the signing of the contract. English courts will impose liability for fraud on such facts, unless in the context it is quite clear to the reasonable recipient of the information that the party who gives it accepts no responsibility for its accuracy or for reviewing it.[143] However there are examples[144] that go further than English law, the *Daktari* film rights case being just one. In cases involving the sale of businesses, the information not disclosed seems to be precisely the sort of thing that in English practice would be the subject of pre-contract enquires or a schedule of warranties.[145]

I have not found it easy to locate discussion of the relevant policy in German law. Indeed, German colleagues told me that I would find little, and so far that has proved to be the case. The discussion is primarily in terms of concepts, for example, the distinction between declaration and motive. At times I thought it was entirely stuck in *Begriffs-jurisprudenz*, the jurisprudence of concepts. That is not true. The rules on mistake show at least the strong influence of *Interressenjurisprudenz*, considerations of balancing of interests. These are demonstrated by the development of *culpa in contrahendo* and the linked policy of protecting reliance that underlies §122. Private law more generally has also been influenced by wider notions of the State's social responsibility, but to what extent the law on mistake and

---

[142] e.g. NJW-RR 2003, 700.

[143] *IFE Fund SA v Goldman Sachs International* [2006] EWHC 2887 (Comm), [2007] 1 Lloyd's Rep. 26 at [60]; [2007] EWCA Civ 811, [2007] 2 Lloyd's Rep. 449, see at [35], [38], and [74].

[144] See Markesinis, 308, giving examples of defects in land; the financial condition of a company sold, see BGH 6 December 1996 (note 138 above)—seller must inform buyer of fall in turnover. It is noticeable that courts not only deny relief when the matter is not so important, but also when question seems an obvious one for C to have asked but did not: BGH 13 July 1988, NJW 1989.763 (trans Ius Commune casebook case no 10.44), so the duty arises where C is not likely to know or to ask about the relevant fact.

[145] NJW 2001, 2163.

non-disclosure has been influenced by this third notion it is very hard to say.

We must not assume that all German lawyers necessarily support the solutions found in their law. § 119(2) has been controversial. Zimmermann quotes a description of the jurisprudence as a 'magical mystery tour';[146] the *Münchener Kommentar* complains that there is still no workable criteria for distinguishing mistakes as to 'essential qualities' from motivational mistakes.[147] The case law on the duty to disclose, and the *Daktari* case[148] in particular, has also been criticized.[149] Others argue that the law is too narrow—for example, Kramer points out that the mistake provisions do not allow for relief in cases of 'calculation mistakes'.[150] The major revamp of the BGB in 2001 gave an opportunity to discuss change, but it was not taken up, nor does it seem to have been considered in the wider review of the BGB which preceded the 2001 reforms.[151] This suggests at least that there is no consensus among German lawyers that there is an overwhelming problem with §§ 119 and 122, or with the way in which duties of disclosure are applied.

---

[146] Zimmermann, *Obligations*, 616, quoting Raape (1949) 150 Archiv für die civilistische Praxis 501.

[147] Munch K (Kramer) § 119, Rnn 102, 105.

[148] See above, p 1, n 2.

[149] e.g. Kötz (above, n 116), 201 (see above, p 29); Markesinis, 309.

[150] Markesinis, 283.

[151] Thus there were no proposals on mistake in the BGB-KE (Abschlussbericht der Kommission zur Überarbeitung des Schuldrechts—Draft provisions proposed by the Commission on the Reform of the Law of Obligations, 1992); the draft concentrated on the provisions on breach of contract and prescription, see W Lorenz, 'Reform of the German law of Breach of Contract' (1997) 1 Edinburgh LR 317, 344; R Zimmermann, *The New German Law of Obligations* (OUP, Oxford, 2005), 31–32. Nor was mistake in contract covered in the extensive studies carried out before the drafting of the BGB-KE: see Bundesminister der Justiz (ed), *Gutachten und Vorschläge zur Überarbeitung des Schuldrechts*, (Vols I and II, 1981; Vol III, 1983, Bundesanzeiger, Köln).

The Netherlands

I will end this brief survey of codified systems with the Dutch Civil Code (BW), as an example of a modern code. Before the current BW came into effect, the courts had developed a doctrine of pre-contractual duty to inform based on good faith.[152]

Article 6:228 of the BW provides that a contract which has been entered into under the influence of error, and which would not have been entered into had there been a correct assessment of the facts, can be annulled for a unilateral mistake that was not caused by the other party, but only 'if the other party, in view of what he knew or ought to know regarding the error, should have informed the party in error'.[153]

If Art 6:228 is representative of modern civilian thinking, it suggests two tendencies. The first is to abandon specific categories of mistake which are or are not treated as relevant and to replace them by a general formula.[154] The distinction between substance and motive has gone.

In a famous Dutch case of 1959, *Stevensweerd Kantharos*,[155] C had sold a cup which he had found. Later it was found to be a very valuable Greco-Roman kantharos. C was not allowed to avoid the contract for mistake, and it is thought that this remains the case under art 6:228: he takes the risk that it may turn out to be valuable, and therefore the mistake is a matter 'for which the party in error should remain accountable'.[156] However, if the buyer was an expert and the seller was not, it is said that the position would be different.[157] What does not seem to matter is the issue in the French *Poussin* case, namely, whether the seller had a

---

[152] Sefton-Green, 151.

[153] For the full article, see Appendix, below, p 133.

[154] Though errors as to future facts are specifically excluded, BW 6:228(2).

[155] HR 19 June 1959.

[156] Art 6:228(2) BW, see Appendix, below, p 133; Sefton-Green, 114.

[157] Sefton-Green, 114 n 115, referring to a number of authors.

positive belief that the item was something different to what it turned out to be—in the French case, an incorrect belief that the painting could not be by Poussin.[158]

The second trend that appears from art 6:228 BW is to limit relief for unilateral mistakes which were not caused by the other party giving incorrect information. This kind of unilateral mistake of itself is no longer a ground for avoidance: under art 6:228(1)(b), relief is limited to cases in which D should have informed C. If C has made a mistake of which D knows, but in the circumstances D is not obliged by good faith[159] to reveal the truth, for example because that would involve D in revealing information which he has gained only at considerable cost,[160] C may not avoid for mistake.

Article 6:228 BW is not easy to interpret. The phrase 'if the other party, in view of what he knew or ought to know regarding the error, should have informed the party in error' has been read as narrowing the circumstances in which relief will be given for unilateral mistake still further. It has sometimes been understood to mean that there will be no relief under this article unless the non-mistaken party knew or at least should have known that the mistake had been made.[161] If D did not know and had no reason to know of C's mistake, how can he be expected to inform C of the error?

However, this seems to be a misunderstanding. The accepted interpretation is that D need know only that the facts or circumstances were essential to the mistaken party,[162] not that C is labouring under a mistake. Indeed, as

---

[158] See the discussion of Sefton-Green's case 2 under Dutch law (150–152); the seller's state of mind seems to be the same as in the *Stevensweerd Kantharos* case.

[159] Or 'opinion generally accepted in society', see below. 'The requirement of good faith is still said to explain why under certain circumstances a party may be under a duty to inform ...': Sefton-Green 151.

[160] See below, p 91.

[161] e.g. PECL, p. 236; H Beale, A Hartkamp, H Kötz and D Tallon, *Cases, Materials and Text on Contract Law* (1st edn, Hart, Oxford, 2002), 394.

[162] See Hartkamp and Tillema, *Contract Law in the Netherlands* (Kluwer, The Hague, 1995), para 80. See Ius Commune casebook, 496; Asser-Hartkamp 6–III* nr 226ff.

in the other civilian systems, if D has actual knowledge of C's mistake there may be liability in fraud for dishonest silence.[163] The point may be that sometimes D is expected to point out facts to C if they are essential to C, whether or not D knows or should know that C is actually labouring under a mistake. If indeed C has made a mistake, and D had not disclosed the facts, C may avoid the contract. This approach in effect creates a prophylactic duty to warn.

The case law that I have seen translated or discussed in English does not provide a clear answer to the question above, nor does it make it clear when there will be a duty to inform. The Hoge Raad has said that parties have a duty to inform themselves of the facts, but that D may have a duty to give information in order to prevent a mistake. Whether the seller must reveal its knowledge, for example that cracks in the building sold are due to inadequate foundations, or may assume that the buyer will investigate the cause, depends on 'opinion generally accepted in society' and the 'particularities of the case'.[164] On the facts of the case it would be hard to argue that the sellers had no reason to suspect the buyer was mistaken.[165] Commentators state that it is difficult to establish when there is a duty to inform.[166]

---

[163] Hartkamp and Tillema, para 80, point out that knowledge would be relevant to a claim for damages under BW art 6:162 (a general provision on liability for damage caused by unlawful acts).

[164] HR 10 April 1998, NJ 1998, 666 with a note by WM Kleijn. This case was decided under the law of the former Dutch civil code, which was in force in the Dutch Antilles at that time, but it is said to reflect present Dutch law with respect to art 6:228 1(b) BW: Asser/Hartkamp 6–III* 2010 nr. 231. Compare HR 14 November 2008, NJ 2008, 588, in which it was held that it was obvious that the beams in a 16th century building might not be adequate for the restaurant that the buyer had in mind, and therefore the buyer's duty to inform itself prevailed over any duty on the seller to reveal what its surveyors had reported. I am indebted to Dr J Rutgers for translations of the cases.

[165] Sefton-Green, 212–213 suggests that the buyer's duty to inform himself will usually be held to outweigh the seller's duty to inform unless the seller had positive knowledge.

[166] Asser/Hartkamp 6–III* 2010 nr 232; Sefton-Green 151.

Nordic laws

The third of the three approaches I mentioned earlier is represented by the Nordic laws. The laws of contract in Denmark, Finland, Norway, and Sweden have much in common because each adopted the so-called 'Nordic Contracts Act.[167] Under the Act, relief on the grounds of mistake itself is limited to cases of mistakes in declaration.[168] There is a provision on fraud which is broad enough to cover fraud by silence,[169] but it is reported to be little used, at least in Sweden.[170]

Instead, the Nordic laws seem to employ two main approaches to the problem with which we are dealing.[171] The first is to treat the non-mistaken party as having failed

---

[167] This was the model for Contracts Acts which entered into force in Sweden (1915), Denmark (1916), Norway (1918) and Finland (1929). For an account of the relevant provisions see T Wilhelmsson, 'Good Faith and the Duty of Diclosure in Commercial Contracting—The Nordic Experience', in R Brownsword, N Hurd and G Howells (eds), *Good Faith in Contract* (Ashgate, Aldershot, 1999), 165.

[168] Section 32.

[169] R Nielsen, *Contract Law in Denmark* (Kluwer, The Hague, 1997), § 369.

[170] R Zimmermann and S Whittaker (eds), *Good Faith in European Contract Law* (CUP, Cambridge, 2000), 233, discussing a case of the buyer's failure to disclose the value (and probably the attribution) of a picture to an obviously ignorant seller. The reporters for Denmark, Finland and Norway do not refer to this section in their accounts.

[171] There is also a doctrine of implied conditions, apparently imported under the influence of Windscheid (see Sefton-Green, 114), which can be used to provide relief, not only in cases of common mistake but also when one party was acting on a crucial assumption which was incorrect, and this assumption was or ought to have been known to the other, even without the other being aware of the first party's mistake: See O Lando, 'The Law of Contracts', in H Gammeltoft-Hansen et al (eds) *Danish Law: a General Survey* (Gads, Copenhagen, 1982), 152 *et seq*. Relief will be given only if the mistaken party is not regarded as taking the risk of its own assumptions: Sefton-Green 115. The doctrine has apparently been used more in Denmark than Sweden, where it is regarded as 'controversial', or in Finland, where it has had only 'limited' acceptance (see DCFR II-7:201, note I.2). Even in Denmark it is said to be replaced by the modern approach looking at fairness, though one commentator remarks that it was thought to be dead but has been revived: B Dahl in B Dahl,

to perform the contract. This is done by employing a broad notion of 'defect' which depends not so much on objective qualities or evaluation of the goods or other property as on what the buyer thought they would receive, provided that the seller knew or should have known of the buyer's expectation. Thus the Danish Sale of Goods Act of 2003 provides:

76. (1) The goods are not in conformity with the contract if...
      (iii) the seller has failed to give the buyer notice of circumstances that influenced the buyer's assessment of the goods and which were known or ought to have been known by the seller...[172]

In similar vein, the Norwegian Sale of Property Act of 1992 provides:

The property has a defect if the purchaser has not been informed about conditions which the seller knew of or could not have been unaware of, and of which the purchaser had reason to believe that he should have been informed. This, however, is only relevant if one could assume that the non-performance has influenced the contract.[173]

Likewise, the Swedish Land Code of 1970, Section 19 provides[174] that the seller will be in breach 'if the property unit... deviates from what the purchaser could have justifiably anticipated at the time of the purchase'. This provision was used by the Swedish Supreme Court to give relief to a buyer of an apartment who was not told by the seller that because of a change in traffic regulations, the apartment would become much noisier.[175]

T Melchior and D Tamms (eds), *Danish Law in a European Perspective* (2nd edn, Forlaget Thomson, Copenhagen, 2002), 250.

[172] Trans: <http://www.sprog.asb.dk/sn/cisg>. See also the Finnish Act (355/1987), s 19, referred to in this context by T Wilhelmsson (above, n 167), 166.

[173] Sale of Property Act, 3 July 1992, no 93, § 3–7, quoted in Sefton-Green, 215.

[174] SFS 1970:994 jordabalk.

[175] NJA 1981.894, cited in Sefton-Green 216.

The second approach is to rely on general clauses. The provision most frequently cited in this context is § 33 of the Nordic Contracts Act:

33. Even if a declaration of intention shall otherwise be regarded as valid, the person to whom the declaration was made may not, however, rely on the declaration if, as a result of circumstances existing at the time when he had notice of the declaration and of which he must be deemed to have known, it would be against the principles of good faith to enforce the declaration.

In the *travaux préparatoires* it was said that the section can be used whenever the promise in a dishonest way took advantage of the promisor's ignorance of the circumstances,[176] for instance by selling shares without revealing that the company is insolvent.[177] In all four jurisdictions it would be the first article of the Nordic Contracts Act under which to deal with the case of a party buying a picture without telling the seller, who was obviously ignorant, that it was by an old master.[178] In Finland[179] § 33 has regularly been relied on as requiring a party to disclose facts that were crucial to the contract but that the other did not know; such as when the seller of a kiosk did not reveal to the buyer that the kiosk would have to be moved,[180] or when a buyer of land knew that the seller was mistaken about the right to build on the land and therefore was allowing it to go for too low a price.[181]

In general, for relief under § 33 it seems that the non-mistaken party must have known the importance of the matter to the other,[182] but it is not necessary that the non-mistaken party was aware of the other's mistake;

---

[176] Sefton-Green, 232.

[177] See Wilhelmsson (above, n 167), 173.

[178] See Zimmermann & Whittaker (above, n 170), 230–3.

[179] See Wilhelmsson (above, n 167), 174. Wilhelmsson also discusses KKO 1985 II 58, a case of selling shares in circumstances that seem to have amounted to insider dealing.

[180] KKO 1949 II 258 (Wilhelmsson, 174).

[181] KKO 1975 II 92 (see Zimmermann & Whittaker (above, n 170), 233).

[182] DCFR art II-7:201, note II.10.

that merely strengthens the case for relief.[183] As the non-mistaken party is at fault, it is said that the mistaken party may alternatively claim damages.[184]

It seems that § 33 can be applied to any error, one of motive,[185] or even of value.[186] The approach is flexible: fault on the part of the mistaken party is only a factor, not a bar to relief. On the other hand, it seems that relief will not be given if the court thinks that the mistaken party should bear the risk of his mistake. Thus in a Swedish case where buyers bid on a picture thinking that it was genuine because it appeared to bear the artist's signature, the seller was not required to point out that it was a reproduction.[187]

§ 33 is sometimes described as being based on fairness rather than good faith.[188] However, the point is frequently made that relief will not be given unless the non-mistaken party should have known of the importance of the mistake, because only then would it be contrary to good faith to insist on the contract.[189] From the discussion, it seems to bite on either procedural or substantive unfairness. But assessments of the practical importance of § 33 seem to vary. Some commentators point out that much of the work is done by the rules on non-conformity described earlier,[190] and that there are not many cases.[191]

There is also § 36, which was introduced into the Acts by later amendments:

---

[183] Sefton-Green 117; DCFR art II-7:201, note II.22 ('must have known' or, in Finland, 'ought to have known').

[184] Sefton-Green, 153, referring to some writers who argue that the damages may include loss of expectation.

[185] DCFR art II-7:201, note VI.28.

[186] DCFR art II-7:201, note VI.30, citing KKO 1968 II 33.

[187] See NJA 1975 152 (Zimmermann & Whittaker (above, n 170), 232).

[188] See Wilhelmsson (above, n 167), 166; Lando (above, n 171), 158.

[189] e.g. C Hultmark, in M Bogdan (ed), *Swedish Law in the New Millennium* (Norstedts Juridik, Stockholm, 2000), 10.8.

[190] Sefton-Green 216.

[191] Thus it is reported that in the Norwegian Supreme Court there were no cases between businesses based on § 33 between 1945 and 1991: Sefton-Green, 260.

36. (1) A contract may be modified or set aside, in whole or in part, if it would be unreasonable or at variance with the principles of good faith to enforce it. The same applies to other juristic acts.

    (2) In making a decision under subsection (1) hereof, regard shall be had to the circumstances existing at the time the contract was concluded, the terms of the contract and subsequent circumstances.

§ 36 can in principle cover cases of mistake, but it does not seem that it has been employed in this context; at any rate, it is suggested that the same factors will be relevant as under § 33.[192]

Lastly, there is a suggestion that a mistaken party may also be able to obtain relief if the other party has not yet relied on the contract.[193]

UNITED STATES

In the US, so far as the laws of the individual states are accurately reflected in the Restatement 2d and the cases cited in leading textbooks, there has been a significant departure from the 'classical' common law model.[194] This has occurred in at least two types of case.

---

[192] Zimmermann & Whittaker (above, n 170), 231.

[193] DCFR art II-7:201, note V.26, on the basis of § 39 of the Act. This provides that:

'[W]hen, under the provisions of this Act, the binding effect of a declaration of intention depends on the fact that the person to whom it was made did not know or ought not to have known a certain matter or otherwise acted in good faith, regard shall be had to what he realised or ought to have realised at the time he had notice of the declaration. If special circumstances so warrant, regard shall also be had to the knowledge he has acquired or ought to have acquired after the time specified above, but before the declaration of intention has a decisive effect on his conduct.'

The DCFR notes that the Danish court has taken this line (U2001.42) but the courts in Sweden have been reluctant to follow.

[194] For a comparison between the US and England, see A Farnsworth, *Alleviating Mistakes: Reversal and Forgiveness for Flawed Perceptions* (Yale University Press, New Haven, 2004), 206.

The first is where a party has submitted a bid to do work or to buy property and the bid is based on a mistake.[195] Not only may the employer not accept the bid if the bid itself—the figure stated—is obviously erroneous,[196] as in English law; in the US, relief is also allowed by many courts when the error was in the underlying calculations or about the amount of work involved.[197] It is allowed both when the employer knew or ought to have known of the mistake,[198] and also when the employer did not know of it when it accepted the bid but the employer has not yet relied on the bid, provided that it would be 'unconscionable' for the employer to insist on performance. Relief may be refused on the ground of reliance if, for example, the employer has relied on the bid by rejecting other bids for the same work and so making it impossible to turn immediately to another contractor. In some courts, relief may be allowed only if the mistaken bidder pays the cost of arranging a second round of tendering.[199] The further requirement that it must be 'unconscionable' to enforce the contract sounds very restrictive, but the cases I have read suggest it is satisfied as soon as it is shown that as the result of the mistake the bidder would make a significant loss on the contract.[200]

[195] See Farnsworth, *Contracts*, 614.

[196] Restatement 2d § 153, Illustration 1 is of a bidder who misses an item in a column of figures so that the total price given at the end is shown as $150,000 instead of $200,000. The Reporter's note gives a long list of authorities.

[197] Farnsworth, 615, referring to cases such as *Boise Junior College District v Mattefs Construction Co*, 450 P 2d 604 (bid failed to include item for glass); Restatement 2d § 153, Illustration 4 is of a bid which is too low because the bidder misinterpreted the employer's specifications.

[198] Farnsworth, 617, citing *Geremia v Boyarsky*, 140 A 749 (Conn 1928). Relief is similarly allowed when the bidder had been misled by the employer's specifications: ibid, citing *Centex Construction Co v James*, 374 F 2d 921 (8th Cir 1967). See Restatement 2d § 153 (b) ('the other party had reason to know of the mistake or his fault caused the mistake').

[199] Farnsworth, 616, citing *Board of Regents of Murray State Normal School v Cole*, 273 SW 508 (Ky 1925).

[200] See e.g. *Crenshaw County Hospital Board v St Paul Fire and Marine Insurance Co*, 411 F 2d 213 (5th Cir 1969); Restatement 2d § 153 Illustration 2.

Relief will sometimes be denied on the basis that the mistaken party should bear the risk of its mistake. This seems to happen when the mistake was 'an error of judgment' rather than a clerical error or some other form of positive mistake;[201] or when the risk is one that the bidder was in a better position to evaluate than the employer.[202]

Relief on similar grounds has also been given in other types of case which seem to involve unilateral mistake as to the facts rather than the price or other terms of the contract,[203] and Restatement 2d states a general rule:

§ *153 When Mistake of One Party Makes a Contract Voidable*
Where a mistake of one party at the time a contract was made as to a basic assumption on which he made the contract has a material effect on the agreed exchange of performances that is adverse to him, the contract is voidable by him if he does not bear the risk under the rule stated in § 154, and
(a) the effect of the mistake is such that enforcement of the contract would be unconscionable, or
(b) the other party had reason to know of the mistake or his fault caused the mistake.

Secondly, despite the authority of *Laidlaw v Organ*,[204] some courts have held that a party who sells property which he knows to be defective in a way that the buyer is not aware of must disclose this to the buyer. A much cited example is *Obde v Schlemeyer*,[205] where the defendants failed to reveal that the house they were selling had suffered from serious termite damage which almost certainly had not been eradicated by the limited treatment they had carried out. They

---

[201] Farnsworth, 616–617, citing *Tony Down Food Co v United States*, 530 F 2d 367 (Ct of Claims 1976).

[202] Thus Restatement 2d § 154 Illustration 6 says relief will be denied if the bid was too low because the bidder has underestimated the labour required to do the work. Unusually, the Reporter's note gives no authority for this Illustration.

[203] e.g. *Beatty v Depue*, 103 NW 2d 187 (SD 1960), a case where the facts again seem almost identical to those of *Denny v Hancock* (1870) LR 6 Ch App 1 (see above, n 48).

[204] 15 US (2 Wheat.) 178 (1817); above, p 17.

[205] 353 P.2d 672 (Wash 1960).

were held liable to the buyers for fraudulent non-disclosure. There is also a direct parallel to the English 'body-parts' case[206] described in Chapter 1: in California it has been held that a seller of a house must disclose the fact that five people had been murdered there.[207] Although it has been said that 'the concept has proved broad enough to give relief for non-disclosure well beyond the termite cases',[208] the cases in which it has been held that there is a duty to disclose all seem to involve a seller who knew of a defect in the property sold.[209] We will see that in cases like *Laidlaw v Organ* itself, the US courts have tended to say that the knowledgeable party need not disclose what he knows.[210]

WHAT TO MAKE OF THIS SURVEY

What can we make of this survey? There are clear differences of approach between the legal systems we have looked at. One is whether the concern is primarily with trying to ensure that a party's consent is informed, at least as regards the facts that are most obviously related to the contract and that are the most important to him or her. Others, like the New Zealand scheme, seem less concerned with the seriousness of the mistake or its obvious relationship to the contract and place the emphasis largely on the

---

[206] *Sykes v Taylor-Rose* [2004] EWCA Civ 299, [2004] 2 P & CR 30.

[207] *Reed v King* 193 Cal Rptr 130 (Cal Ct App 1983).

[208] Farnsworth, 241. At 240 the same author states that where a non-disclosure is unintentional, as when it is due to inadvertence or forgetfulness, it amounts to a non-fraudulent misrepresentation and will give a right to avoidance if it is material; but no authority is given. Writers have frequently argued for a general duty to disclose, subject to exceptions: e.g. M Eisenberg, 'Disclosure in Contract Law' (2003) 91 Calif LR 1645 and the references therein. See further below, pp 91–93.

[209] In *AMPAT/Midwest v Illinois Tool Works* 896 F 2d 1035 (7th Cir 1990), Posner J said that a seller who knows that a problem is caused by a defect in the product cannot keep silent. This appears to relate to a post-contractual situation but presumably the judge thought the seller would also have a pre-contractual duty to disclose known defects.

[210] See below, p 91.

fairness of the resulting exchange. Overall fairness also seems to be an important factor in Scandinavian law, though the relevant sections of the Nordic Contracts Act cover procedural fairness as well as the substantive equality of the exchange.

While in the civilian traditions the notion of informed consent seems to be the basis of relief, the consequences are worked out rather differently. On the face of it French law seems little concerned with protection of the defendant's reliance, whereas in German Law the non-mistaken party's reliance on the mistaken party's promise will be protected provided that it was reasonable. It is possible that in practice the difference is less than it appears because the French courts can employ the rule that the mistake must not be *'inexcusable'* to exclude relief at least when the mistaken party was at fault, and some commentators have said that the courts will apply this rule even in cases of simple negligence: the negligence does not have to be gross to be *inexcusable*.[211] But that can only be an indirect form of protection. It will not help the non-mistaken party who has relied on the contract when the mistaken party was not negligent. The contrast with §§ 119 and 122 BGB is clear: in German law the contract may be avoided but the 'innocent' non-mistaken party will be protected.

Be that as it may, both systems will allow avoidance where the fact that the claimant was mistaken was unknown to the defendant. In contrast, both the PECL and the UPICC limit relief for C's unilateral mistakes to the case where D knew or ought to have known of the mistake. In the case of the PECL, this seems to represent a compromise rather than a common position among the laws of the Member States.[212] Both sets of principles seem to move significantly away from the civilian position towards

---

[211] Ghestin *La Formation du contrat* (above, n 73), no 523.
[212] See H Beale, 'The DCFR: Mistake and Duties of Disclosure' (2008) 4 European Review of Contract Law 317.

protecting the reasonable expectations of the non-mistaken party.[213]

But in all these systems, where the defendant actually knew C was making a mistake but dishonestly decided to say nothing, C may avoid the contract and may claim damages for fraud. Both French and German law also place a duty to inform on parties who have information to which the other is unlikely to have access or which the other may not think to ask about—for example because the parties' relationship is such that the claimant expected to be told of any problem.

Thus what the European models all have in common is that they allow relief in cases in which English law definitely does not. The number of situations that cause problems in practice may not be large, but the differences are remarkable. We might caricature the difference by saying that conduct which on the continent is regarded as fraud is regarded in England as good business.[214]

So we should decide whether we wish to retain our law as it is, or should pursue something closer to the PECL or one of the other models. We should begin by considering whether we can devise an alternative model that will work tolerably well; if we can, we must then decide whether or not we want to adopt it. Those are the issues for Chapter 3.

---

[213] Thus Huber, in S Vogenauer and J Kleinheisterkamp (eds), *Commentary on the UPICC* (OUP, Oxford, 2009), 3.5/3, describes the UPICC article as 'towards the restrictive end of the spectrum', as it emphasizes the reliance of the other party rather than protecting the true will of the mistaken party. UPICC art 3.2.2(1)(b) also permits avoidance for relevant mistake where 'the other party had not at the time of avoidance reasonably acted in reliance on the contract'. See further below, pp 79–80.

[214] Similarly, Farnsworth, 242 quotes *Blair v National Security Insurance Co* 126 F 2d 955, 958 (3d Cir 1942): 'I can buy my neighbour's land for a song, although I know and he doesn't that it is oil-bearing. That isn't dishonest, it is "smart business" and the just reward for my superior individualism.' In the next chapter we will see that non-disclosure may be justified on the facts posited, but not simply on the ground given.

3

Possible Models for
English Law

In the first two chapters of this book I compared the English law on mistake and non-disclosure of facts to various other models. I suggested that despite the many exceptions, there are significant differences between the English law on the one hand, and continental systems, together with those of New Zealand, the US, and to some extent Canada, on the other. The 'residual rule' of English law is fundamentally different to the other systems.

I argued that, at least in principle, some change is desirable. There are cases in which the current law seems quite simply both unfair and inefficient: the obvious 'calculation mistake', as in *The Harriette N*,[1] and the case of the crucial fact known to one party but not the other, as in the US case of *Obde v Schlemeyer*[2] or the German *Daktari* case[3] about film rights.

I argued that a change in the law would be most significant in certain types of transaction. If lack of information about a particular point is something that recurs on a regular basis, lawyers develop practices to overcome the problem.[4] Leaving aside the 'obvious calculation error' cases, the changes I suggest would have an impact primarily in cases involving unusual risks;[5] or where the mistaken party was not sophisticated enough to realize that it should take

---

[1] *Statoil ASA v Louis Dreyfus Energy Services LP (The Harriette N)* [2008] EWHC 2257 (Comm), [2008] 2 Lloyd's Rep. 685, above, p 1.

[2] 353 P.2d 672 (Wash 1960); above, p 70.

[3] BGH 31 January 1979, LM § 123 BGB Nr 52 (trans Markesinis case no 92), above, pp 1 and 29.

[4] See above, pp 24–26.

[5] As in *Sykes v Taylor-Rose* [2004] EWCA Civ 299 (the 'body parts' case), above, p 27.

advice, or thought that the cost of advice would not be justified; or where the mistaken party's relationship to the other party to the contract was such that they were lulled into a false sense of security.[6]

In this third chapter, I will consider two questions:

(1) If we are to consider a different model, what model would be the most plausible? Before we decide whether we want any change we need to see if we can develop a workable model, one that will produce 'right' results in a variety of situations without creating an unacceptable degree of uncertainty.

(2) Do we want to adopt the model? This involves asking, what kind of contract law do we want?

MODELS NOT TO FOLLOW

There are some approaches which I think we need not pursue. For example, I would not suggest following the broadbrush approach used in the Nordic laws. Sections 33 and 36 of the Nordic Contracts Act[7] require the courts to decide whether the contracts should be enforced according to the very broad test of good faith. Even though colleagues tell me that the courts apply these sections sparingly, I cannot see such a broad and unstructured discretion being acceptable to judges, let alone practitioners, in this country.[8] For the same reason I would also suggest that we do not follow the model of the New Zealand Contractual Mistakes Act 1977. It too leaves so much to the court's discretion.[9]

---

[6] As in the *Daktari* case, above, n 3.

[7] See above, p 66.

[8] Nor would I follow the other Nordic approach of widening the contractual obligations of the seller: see above, pp 64–65. It does not seem necessary to impose additional contractual obligations, of uncertain extent, on the seller.

[9] See above, p 40.

We need to develop a model that gives relief according to more closely-defined criteria.

THE UNDERLYING AIM: PROTECTION OF AUTONOMY OR FAIRNESS IN EXCHANGE?

First, we need to decide on the underlying aim of any reform. It has been pointed out that the NZ Contractual Mistakes Act seems to be driven by the notion that what matters is whether the exchange that resulted from the contract was a fair one.[10] In contrast, the other systems—particularly the civilian systems[11]—concentrate on whether the party's consent to the contract was fully informed. It seems to me that the 'informed consent' model is the one to follow. Whether we think of the enforcement of contract as resting on the moral principle that promises should be performed,[12] or on the need to support exchanges that will leave both parties better off (and thus increase the wealth of society generally),[13] it is the fact that the promisor was mistaken or not fully informed which suggests that their promise should not bind them.[14] The important point is not that the exchange should be at roughly the

[10] See Contractual Mistakes Act 1977 s 6(1)(b)(i), above, p 40; Beck, 'The New Zealand Contractual Mistakes Act: a lesson in legislation' [1987] LMCLQ 325, 326; D L Lange, 'Statutory Reform of the Law of Mistake' (1980) 18 Osgoode Hall LJ 428.

[11] Some Nordic writers have argued that relief for mistake under the Contracts Act should aim to protect autonomy rather than fairness: see O Lando (above, p 64, n 171), 155; R Nielsen (above, p 64, n 169) § 360.

[12] See e.g. C Fried, *Contract as Promise: A Theory of Contractual Obligation* (Harvard University Press, Cambridge Mass., 1981).

[13] e.g. A Kronman and R Posner, *Economics of Contract Law* (Little Brown, Boston, 1979), 4.

[14] Fried (above, n 12) at 81: ' ... where the parties have not intended to undertake an allocation of risk, the mere fact that the general words of what they have undertaken appear to cover an unexpected case should not of itself bind them in that case. There has been a mistake ... unilateral mistake presents the weaker case for relief, especially where one party is simply trying to enforce what he thought the bargain was. But *Obde* is not like that ... when one of the parties causes the accident ... (as in *Obde*), the equities quite clearly do not favour him.'

market price but that if one party was mistaken, the moral case for holding him to his promise is less strong, particularly if the mistake was known to the other party. Equally, we can no longer presume that the agreement would be value-maximizing for both parties.[15] Of course arguments can be made for setting aside contracts that are seriously unbalanced in terms of value for money,[16] but policing contracts for fairness of price is far removed from current English legal thinking. It would also involve questions well beyond mistake.

A PLAUSIBLE 'INFORMED CONSENT' MODEL

So, following the 'informed consent' model, let me begin with relief for unilateral mistake. I think it will help to consider two different aspects of the problem in turn. I will start by considering the strength of the claim by the non-mistaken party (D) that her reliance should be protected, and then consider the nature of the mistake that the mistaken party, the claimant (C), has made.

D's claim for protection of reliance or expectation

Let us suppose C has made a mistake which is serious; had C known the truth, he would never have agreed to the contract. Let us also assume that D had no justification for withholding the information from C (a point to which I will return).[17]

D's claim that her interest should be protected is clearly strongest when she did not know, and had no reason to know, of C's mistake. The claim is weaker if D should have known that C had or might well have made a mistake, and

---

[15] Kronman and Posner (above, n 13) suggest that liability is imposed to deter careless behaviour.

[16] See e.g. J Gordley, 'Equality in Exchange' (1981) 69 Calif LR 1583.

[17] See below, p 91.

weakest when D had actual knowledge that C was making a mistake.

Where D did not know and had no reason to know of the mistake English law, and indeed the common law throughout the world, has a tradition of giving strong protection to reliance. However, our survey has shown that there are different means of achieving this. Whereas the traditional common law approach is simply to treat C's mistake as irrelevant, in German law C is permitted to avoid the contract but on condition that D is compensated for her reliance loss under § 122 BGB. Section 122 applies unless D knew or should have known of the ground for avoidance, in other words unless D's reliance was not justifiable.[18]

The German approach is in many ways attractive. It seems eminently logical. If C's error was sufficiently serious that he would never have entered the contract, we can no longer justify enforcement of the contract on the grounds that it is necessarily a value-maximizing exchange. Rather, economists argue that any liability should be tort-like, for misleading D.[19] In contrast, the English solution of simply holding the mistake to be irrelevant, so that the contract is fully binding, seems over-protective.[20] It does more than protect D's reliance: it gives D her expectation. The German approach is also more nuanced than the approach of the US cases,[21] and also of the UPICC, which

[18] In contrast, in France, though in principle a mistaken party who was careless and who by appearing to consent caused the other party loss might be liable to pay compensation under art 1382 CC, I understand that this is very rare in practice, possibly because a party whose mistake was sufficiently inexcusable will be denied relief in the first place; see above, p 45.

[19] See n 13 above.

[20] This has been recognized judicially by Franks J in *Ricketts v Pennsylvania Rly Co* 153 F 2d 757, 766–767. The judge points out that reliance loss should include loss of opportunity to make another bargain. Cf L Fuller and W Perdue, 'The Reliance Interest in Contract Damages' (1936) 46 Yale LJ 52, 62 and A Farnsworth, *Alleviating Mistakes* (see above, p 68, n 194) 168 (expectation loss awarded because reliance loss too hard to establish).

[21] See above, p 69.

is to allow avoidance unless there has been reliance.[22] Allowing relief when there has been no reliance seems to be a compromise; but I am not clear that it has other merits.[23] There will always have been some degree of reliance, if only the cost of reading the claimant's bid.[24] Moreover, it is an 'on/off' test: the reliance 'trigger' seems unrelated to the extent of D's loss if avoidance is permitted, and to the amount of C's loss if it is not. The US cases leave a good deal of uncertainty over the extent of the reliance that must have taken place and the UPICC do not address the issue. This approach does not seem worth pursuing.

What the current English approach has is the merit of simplicity. It is very much easier to state the parties' obligations—quite simply, C must perform—and, if C does perform, it avoids difficult questions of proving and calculating D's losses—issues that are likely to be particularly difficult if D claims that C caused it to lose the opportunity to make another contract with someone else. As recent misrepresentation cases show,[25] the court may end up having to work out the chances that D would have been able to make an alternative deal. Moreover, the English approach is consistent with its approach when C's mistake was in stating the terms of its offer: a mistake of which D did not know and had no reason to know is irrelevant.[26] A third argument is that the English rule gives a stronger ideological message to potential contractors: find out the facts for yourself, by

---

[22] UPICC 2010, art 3.2.2(1)(b).

[23] Huber (above, p 73, n 213) 3.5/25 reports that the provision was inserted at a later stage and has been criticized.

[24] Huber 3.5/23 argues that the cost of making the contract is not sufficient reliance to prevent avoidance.

[25] *4Eng Ltd v Harper* [2008] EWHC 915 (Ch), [2009] Ch 91; *Parabola Investments Ltd v Browallia Cal Ltd* [2009] EWHC 901 (Comm) at [147]. (The Court of Appeal held that the issue of loss of chance did not arise on the facts: [2010] EWCA Civ 486 at [23].)

[26] *Centrovincial Estates Plc v Merchant Investors Assurance Co Ltd* [1983] Com LR 158. In 'mistake in the declaration' cases, German law again allows the mistaken party to avoid the contract whether or not the other party knew of the mistake (§ 119(1) BGB), subject to paying D compensation for its reliance losses (§ 122 BGB).

asking the other party or in some other way. Stand on your own two feet.

Thus we should rule out relief on the ground of mistake as to the facts where D does not know and has no reason to know that C has made a mistake.[27]

D knows of C's mistake

At the other end of the scale are the cases in which D had actual knowledge of C's mistake, or C's ignorance of the relevant fact, and of its crucial relevance. Later I will argue that there are some cases of this type in which D should not be required to point out C's mistake or reveal information that C does not have, but in cases like *The Harriette N* and *Obde*, D's reliance, let alone D's expectation, seem unworthy of protection. Our current rule seems to be indefensible unless it can be justified on some other ground. I suggest that there are only two plausible grounds. One is that any alternative model is unworkable. It is too early to answer that question. The other is that there is such a strong need for market discipline, to encourage parties to take greater care in their calculations or in making enquiries, that we are prepared to ignore the weakness of the defendant's case for protection.

We normally want contracting parties to take steps to inform themselves because they are able to make enquiries and they are in a better position than the other party to know what is important to them. Thus if we ask, who should bear the risk of a mistake of this kind, the answer is that the person who needs the information should do so, because they are the least cost avoider. They should bear the risk so as to give them the incentive to make enquiries.[28] However, it is not always the case that the party to whom the information is crucial is the least cost avoider. In *The Harriette N*[29]

---

[27] Later I argue that this approach also helps to solve the question whether relief should be allowed in cases of mistakes of motive.

[28] Compare Posner and Rosenfield, 'Impossibility and Related Doctrines in Contract Law; an Economic Analysis' (1977) JLS 83, 92.

[29] Above, n 1.

there is little doubt that the mistake was the 'fault' of the sellers. Initially at least, the sellers were the least cost avoiders. But once the mistake has been made, that is no longer the case, at least where D knows of the mistake. This will also apply in the *Obde*-type case. So efficiency demands that if C has made a mistake and D knows it, the burden of preventing the mistake affecting the contract should now be placed on D—in other words, D should have to point out C's mistake to him.

True, it is possible that if you know that the other party will have a duty to point out mistakes of which they become aware, you will have a reduced incentive to take care in the first place. But the effect seems likely to be slight. You will still have a strong incentive to make enquiries, since there is no certainty that the existence of your mistake will become known to the other party and so trigger the duty to point it out.

So in the case in which D actually knows that C has made a crucial mistake, I find the market discipline argument very weak. The same applies when D was reckless, in the sense of knowing that there is a high risk that C has made a mistake and deliberately doing nothing.

What I am arguing, then, is that (with certain exceptions which I will discuss later) there is a strong case for relief in cases of deliberate or reckless silence.

D should have known

It is the intermediate cases that are difficult. First, what if D knew of C's mistake, or that C was ignorant of a fact, but was not aware of the importance of the matter to C? Secondly, what if D knew how important the matter was to C, but did not know that C was mistaken?

When we considered the civilian systems in Chapter 2, we saw that they normally require that D knew or should have known of the importance of the matter to C—put in crude terms, it must be either something that is 'objectively' important, i.e. would be important to most parties, or something that D knew to be 'subjectively' important to C. However, the systems do not require that D knew or should have known that C was in fact mistaken. At first this distinction seems puzzling but I think it makes some sense. If D knows how important something is to C, it requires little effort on her part to check that C is properly informed. If on the other hand D has no reason to think that the information is important, she is unlikely to raise the issue. It seems right to give relief in cases in which D knew or should have known of the importance of the information to C,[30] but not if D had no reason to know of its importance.

What is less obvious is whether relief should be allowed for a mistake of this kind when D did not realize that C was in fact mistaken—but D should have known. In many of these situations (particularly in the 'mistaken calculation' cases), there will be a degree of fault on both sides, so D's moral claim for protection is certainly stronger than in the case where he actually knew of the mistake. But if D should have known both that C was mistaken or did not know a fact and that the matter was of crucial importance, it seems arguable that C should have a right to avoid the contract, as would be the case under German law.

I have not found it easy to reach a conclusion on this point and I am going to leave it as an open question. In what follows I will pursue what rules we might need if we were to go down that route.

There is a third difficult case. We have seen that French, German, and Dutch law all now impose a prophylactic duty to warn, when one party has or should have information that the other is most unlikely to have and would have difficulty in obtaining. This does not depend on proof that D knew C was mistaken, nor that D should have known that on the facts the individual claimant was mistaken. It is at most a case in which C 'might well' have made a mistake. Would we wish to adopt something similar? I think that as a general principle, if D has or should have critical information that the other is most unlikely to have and would have difficulty in obtaining, it may be wise

---

[30] I would apply this even when D actually knew of C's mistake or ignorance.

to impose an obligation of disclosure. C never was the least cost avoider, never was in a better position to find out the truth. However, I am not convinced that we should enact this principle as a rule of law. It may be better to proceed in the typically English fashion of imposing such a duty only in particular cases that have proved problematic[31]—as to some extent has already been done, for example by the provisions of the Sale of Goods Act 1979 considered in Chapter 1.[32]

The nature of C's mistake

I turn now to C's perspective and consider the nature of the mistake that might give rise to relief (again leaving for later consideration that there may be some kinds of information that D should be entitled to keep to herself). The essential point I want to address here is that if any mistake, even one that seems relatively minor, is to be treated as a ground for relief, there may be damage to the notion of the binding force of contract, and it might cause too much uncertainty. It would be possible to dispense with any requirement that the mistake be of a particular seriousness and simply to give the court a very broad discretion as to whether to grant relief and as to the form of relief. In the interest of retaining at least some certainty, I think it would be better to give C a right to avoid the contract only if more precise conditions are met.

Fundamental mistakes
We do not need an elaborate discussion of the kind of mistake on C's part that should qualify for relief. It seems to me that the requirement that the mistake be as to

---

[31] Waddams also favours an incremental approach: S Waddams, 'Pre-contractual Duties of Disclosure' in P Cane and J Stapleton (eds), *Essays for Patrick Atiyah* (Clarendon Press, Oxford, 1991), 237.
[32] See above, p 21.

'substantial qualities' of the subject-matter, or to the qualities that are 'regarded as essential in business', even though they may have had a different importance originally, are nowadays expressions of two requirements: first, the mistake should be serious to the mistaken party; and, secondly, the matter we have explored already—namely, the importance of the matter—should be sufficiently apparent to the non-mistaken party.

The first requirement was addressed in Roman law by requiring that the mistake be one of a list.[33] Over time the old Roman categories were replaced by more general notions such as 'substantial qualities of the subject matter'. Now the idea that the mistake must go to the subject-matter of the contract is in turn being replaced by more general tests, as in BW art 6:228.[34]

The second requirement is intertwined with causation. It would clearly not be right to give relief for a mistake which did not in fact influence C's decision to enter the contract. In addition, as we saw earlier, it is common to restrict relief to cases in which D knew or ought to have known that the relevant mistake would influence C. In practice, this is likely to restrict relief to cases of a certain seriousness, and it is notable that BW art 6:228 contains no separate requirement that the mistake be in some way fundamental.

That is no doubt sufficient in a system which is used to dealing with mistakes in this way. If we are to introduce wider relief for mistake in English law, it should be confined to cases in which the mistake is—and is or should be known to be—serious. We might well adopt the approach of the PECL: the mistake must be such that, had he known the truth, C would not have entered the contract at all or would have done so only on fundamentally different terms.[35]

---

[33] See Zimmermann, *Obligations*, 587 *et seq.*
[34] Quoted in full in Appendix, below, p 133.
[35] PECL art 4:103(1)(b).

Mistakes in motive

Should we exclude mere errors in motive? In the civilian systems the distinction between errors as to substance and errors in motive has been more persistent than others. However, the notion of motive is now treated flexibly, so even an error by one party as to a fact affecting its motives may provide ground for relief if the matter was 'agreed with' or even simply known to the other.[36] Thus B's mistake about whether it will be able to use the land it is buying from S for building may suffice even if S has no interest one way or the other in B's development (except so far as it may affect the price B is willing to pay.)[37]

It is difficult to know where to draw the line. Some of the cases explained on this ground do seem to reach the right result; for example, the case of the woman who buys herself a wedding dress not knowing that her fiancé has just married someone else. One distinction between this and the 'constructability' cases, for example, is that the mistake does not relate in any way to the nature of the property sold, but that distinction can seem a little artificial, for example when the mistake is about whether the buyer will be allowed to build on a piece of land. Fortunately, for the purposes of our scheme, I do not think we have to worry about the distinction between subject-matter and motive. Typically an error in motive will not be apparent to the other party. If we are going to confine relief to cases in which D knows or should know not only of the importance of the matter but also that C has made a mistake, most of the cases that the civilian systems will reject on the ground that the mistake was merely as to motive will fail on the different ground that D will have no idea or reason to know that C is labouring under a mistake. I see no need for a specific exclusion of errors in motive.

In other words, what should matter is not what C was mistaken about; it is whether D knew or should have

---

[36] See above, pp 44–55.
[37] See Nicholas, 92–93.

known that, but for the mistake, C would only have concluded the contract on fundamentally different terms or would not have concluded a contract at all. If these conditions are satisfied, and if D knew (or possibly should have known) that C had made a mistake, the starting point should be that C should have a right to avoid the contract. Thus I think we could go directly to the kind of formulation used in the first paragraph of art 4:103 of the PECL, or in art II – 7:201 of the DCFR, which formulates it more clearly:

> (1) A party may avoid a contract for mistake of fact or law existing when the contract was concluded if:
>   (a) the party, but for the mistake, would not have concluded the contract or would have done so only on fundamentally different terms and the other party knew or could reasonably be expected to have known this; and
>   (b) the other party:
>   (i) ...;
>   (ii) knew or could reasonably be expected to have known of the mistake...

Mistakes about value

Mistakes simply as to value are more problematic. The exclusion of mistakes as to value is useful in some ways because it prevents relief being given in cases in which we are likely to be dealing with a purely distributional question: I sold the dim and dusty painting for £20 because it was worth less to me as a source of pleasure than other things that I can buy with the £20, even if the painting is worth millions to others. Moreover the English tradition is that parties who are not 'specially disadvantaged' should take responsibility for deciding on the appropriate price. Instead of allowing contract prices to be challenged, we have developed non-legal mechanisms to make it easy to find out the value of what you are buying or selling— valuation services, monthly guides to the prices of used vehicles, and records of prices paid for books and works of art at auction. That argues for a bright-line rule: mistakes as to value should not count.

The difficulty is that to exclude mistakes as to value creates borderline problems: was my mistake merely as to the value of the painting, or was my mistake that I thought it could not possibly be by a certain artist?[38] But the distinction between value and characteristics that affect value makes sense. Expecting a party to find out the value of the picture for itself assumes the party knows what he is dealing with. You can't look up the current prices of pictures in auction records if you have the wrong artist. So I am inclined to exclude matters of value from the grounds for relief. In the PECL there is no express exclusion of mistakes as to value but it is said that a mistake as to value is 'not usually fundamental'.[39] That seems an artificial explanation, given that the contract price and the true value may be very different. Perhaps a mistake as to value is better treated as one of the risks that a party should normally bear. Simply for clarity, I think an explicit exception would be better.

Fraud by silence?
At this point, however, there is a complication. So far I have been discussing the seriousness requirement as if the only question were relief on the ground of mistake. Insofar as we are dealing with cases in which D 'should have known', these limits are undoubtedly relevant. However, in French law at least, if D actually knows of C's mistake and deliberately keeps quiet in order that C remains deceived, the case will be one of fraud by silence.[40] Where there is fraud, the limits on relief are removed. Thus where there has been fraud the contract may be avoided even though the resulting mistake was to motive rather than as to substance[41] or was only one as to value.[42]

---

[38] As was the ground for relief in the *Poussin* case, above, p 43.

[39] PECL art 4:103 Comment G.

[40] e.g. Cass Civ 3, 2 October 1974, Bull civ III.330, D1974, IR.252; RGLJ 1975.569, ann Blanc (trans Ius Commune casebook no 10.41); see above, p 46.

[41] For France see above, p 47 and for Germany p 55; see also H Kötz, *European Contract Law* (Clarendon Press, Oxford, 1997), 196.

[42] Malaurie, no 511; K Larenz and M Wolf, *Allgemiener Teil des bürgerlichen Rechts*, (9th edn, Beck, Munich, 2004), § 36 n 55.

When D's failure to disclose was deliberate, an attempt to ensure that C did not discover the truth, should C's error still have to be 'fundamental' or serious? The PECL do not require this: the contract may be avoided for fraud without showing that the mistaken party's error was fundamental. However, under the PECL, as in German law, there will be fraud by keeping silent only when, as a matter of good faith, there is a duty to disclose. For reasons I will explain later, it is likely that any relief would have to be subject to a general test of this kind. It seems unlikely that any English court would say there is a duty unless the information to be disclosed is of fundamental importance. Moreover, to move from a position in which there is no fraud without some form of positive misrepresentation[43] to one in which it would amount to fraud to take deliberate advantage of even a minor mistake would be a very large shift, a step too far, for English law. So I see no need for a special rule for deliberate non-disclosure.

The proposal so far
So let me state my 'provisional proposal' as I have developed it so far. It is that relief should be given if

(i) C, but for the mistake, would only have concluded the contract on fundamentally different terms or would not have concluded a contract at all, and

(ii) D knew both of the importance of the matter to C and that C had actually made mistake; and

(iii) C's mistake is not merely one as to value.

I would suggest also, but more hesitantly, two further extensions: (1) to cases in which D did not actually know of the importance of the matter to C but where, in the circumstances, D should have known of it; and (2) to cases in which D did not know that C had actually made a mistake but in which D should have known it.

---

[43] i.e. not even a misleading half-truth or a statement that was true when made but which became untrue before the time of contract.

Other limits?

Fault of the mistaken party?

In French law[44] and in the PECL,[45] mistake is not a ground for relief if it was inexcusable. If relief is to be limited to cases in which D actually knew of C's mistake, I do not think that a rule of this kind is needed. The fact that C was careless seems irrelevant. The Comments to the PECL in fact say that a careless mistake should not be treated as inexcusable if it was known to the non-mistaken party.[46]

If we were to extend the scheme to the 'should have known of the mistake' cases, then some balancing of relative blame is perhaps inevitable. Fault should not necessarily be a bar to avoidance but we might want to consider damages to compensate D's reliance.[47] But as there would be fault on both sides, questions of causation and contributory negligence would rear their ugly heads. The difficulty and uncertainty that would result may be a very good reason for limiting our reform to the case where D knew of C's mistake.

Risks that should be borne by the mistaken party

This restriction is very common and, I think, useful. There are certain categories of contract where parties knowingly take the risk of mistakes being made. Waddams gives the example of secondhand bookshops: booksellers know that many buyers only come to the shop in the hope of finding treasures that the bookseller has overlooked.[48] Financial markets are another example. Retail financial markets are already covered by legislation[49] and should be excluded for that reason; other financial markets should probably be excluded as areas of known risk.

---

[44] Malaurie, no 506.
[45] PECL art 4:103(2)(a).
[46] PECL art 4:103, Comment I.
[47] I consider the issue of remedies below, p 95.
[48] Waddams (above n 31), 239.
[49] See above, pp 23–24.

Information that D need not disclose

Whether relief is to be given on the ground of fraud or for mistake, there are certain types of information that D should not have to disclose. There are at least two relevant categories: personal information which C is not entitled to ask about and 'productive' information which D obtained only by incurring significant expense.

C should not have to reveal personal information which it would be unlawful for D to take into account, for example where to do so would be discriminatory under the Equality Act 2010. In Germany the courts have held that if D asks about a prospective female employee's pregnancy, she has 'a right to lie'.[50] Clearly there should be no duty to disclose such information.

Kronman's argument[51] that a party should not have to disclose information which he obtained only by incurring significant expense is well known and widely accepted by academic writers.[52] The information does not have to be disclosed, because otherwise D will have no incentive to acquire it in the first place. Thus in the case put by Cockburn CJ[53] there should be no obligation to disclose that minerals have been discovered under the land since to force disclosure would remove the incentives for prospecting and valuable resources would never be unearthed. In contrast, the argument runs, in mistaken bid cases, and even in *Obde*, D acquired the information at no cost and should therefore be required to disclose it. This is consistent with decisions in the US: it seems that the cases that have

---

[50] For details see Markesinis, 304–305 and BAG NZA 2003, 848 (trans Markesinis case no 90).

[51] A Kronman, 'Mistake Disclosure, Information and the Law of Contracts' (1978) 7 JLS 1.

[52] By academic writers even within Europe: e.g. Kötz, (above, n 41), 200; B Rudden, 'Le juste et l'inefficace, Pour un devoir de non-renseignements' (1985) Rev trim dr civ 91. The argument has been adopted judicially in the US by, perhaps not surprisingly, Posner J in *Market St Associates v Frey* 941 F2d 588 (7th Cir 1991), 594.

[53] See above, p 18.

required disclosure are ones in which the seller was aware of a defect in the property being sold,[54] or are ones involving 'calculation' errors.[55]

Since Kronman wrote there have been many analyses of the issue from a broadly similar perspective.[56] A number of reservations to the argument for permitting non-disclosure have emerged,[57] and one of them we must discuss.[58] This is that D should not be entitled to withhold information, even information that was costly for her to acquire, if the information is merely 'foreknowledge', i.e. information that sooner or later will be known by everyone,[59] or is not

---

[54] See A Farnsworth, § 4.11. See also the cases listed in Eisenberg, 'Disclosure in Contract Law' (2003) 91 Calif LR 1645, 1678–1680. Disclosure is also required in case of insider trading: ibid, 1681.

[55] See above pp 37 and 69.

[56] These include: M Trebilcock, *The Limits of Freedom of Contract* (Harvard University Press, Cambridge Mass., 1993), chapter 5; R Cooter and T Ulen, *Law and Economics* (1987; now 6th edn, Addison-Wesley, Boston, 2012) 279–283; R Birmingham, 'The Duty to Disclose and the Prisoner's Dilemma; Laidlaw v Organ' (1988) 29 Wm & Mary LR 249; S Shavell, 'Acquisition and Disclosure of Information Prior to Sale' (1994) 25 Rand J Econ 20; R Barnett, 'Rational Bargaining Theory and Contract: Default Rules, Hypothetical Consent, the Duty to Disclose, and Fraud' (1992) 15 Harv J L & Pub Pol 783; M Eisenberg, 'Disclosure in Contract Law' (2003) 91 Calif LR 1645; O Grosskopf and B Medina, 'A Revised Economic Theory of Duties of disclosure and Break-up fees in Contract Law' (2007) 13 Stanford J Law, Business and Finance 148; M Borden, 'Mistake and Disclosure in a Model of Two-sided Informational Inputs' (2008) 73 Missouri LR 667.

[57] There is also a possible reservation if the information itself was acquired by D without cost but the knowledge to spot its relevance and act on it was costly to acquire (e.g. D by chance hears or spots information which only his expertise allows him to put to good use). Trebilcock (113) argues that the party who acquired the information costlessly must still be encouraged to use it. Eisenberg reasons that though requiring disclosure in this case might have a marginal impact on the incentive to acquire the skill, it will be so slight that it does not justify an exception from the Disclosure Principle for which he argues; and that though D might be dissuaded from making any contract with C if forced to disclose the information, there will usually be other incentives to do so: 1658–1661.

[58] The point is one mentioned very briefly by Kronman, see Eisenberg at 1667.

[59] This approach was suggested by an article by J Hirshleifer, 'The Private and Social Value of Information and the Reward to Inventive Activity' (1971) 61 Am Econ Rev 561.

productive, if having it does not enable a more efficient use of resources but merely gives D a temporary advantage. For example, even if the buyer in *Laidlaw* had incurred expense in building up an extensive network of contacts to acquire early political or other information that might affect the market,[60] it merely gave him a few hours' prior knowledge. That enabled him to make a large profit but the gain was purely distributional; the information did not lead to a more efficient use of resources. Thus Cooter and Ulen argue that contracts that are based on 'purely redistributive information' that was not disclosed should be set aside.[61] The issues are thoroughly discussed by Eisenberg, who concludes that though in a perfect world the Cooter and Ulen test is probably preferable, the test of whether the information is merely foreknowledge 'would be easier to administer in the great majority of disclosure cases, and would probably pick up most of the cases covered by Cooter and Ulen's redistributive category'. In general this seems a sensible qualification of Kronman's argument. It probably does not matter which test is the more accurate. Legislative provisions will seldom work if they seek to be too precise. It would probably be best to apply a general test, such as whether it was compatible with good faith and fair dealing not to disclose the information, and supplement it with guidelines of the general kind found in PECL art 4:107. The two ways of expressing it could be stated as alternatives. I will only remark that to apply this criterion to financial markets might cause no little upset. At least if the Chairman of the FSA is right about the social utility of much of the activity of the sector,[62] players in financial markets

---

[60] In fact it seems that the buyer got his information from acquaintances who had 'insider knowledge' of the negotiations: see J Kaye, 'Disclosure, Information, the Law of Contracts, and the Mistaken Use of *Laidlaw v. Organ*' (2010) 79 Mississippi LJ 577.

[61] Cooter and Ulen (above, n 56), 279–283.

[62] *The Turner Review: A regulatory response to the global banking crisis* (FSA, 2009), 49: '...it seems likely that some and perhaps much of the structuring and trading activity involved in the complex version of securitised credit, was not required to deliver credit intermediation

might have to disclose much hard-won information because the information is unlikely to lead to efficiency gains. The potential for argument about what is or is not 'productive' information, and the resulting uncertainty, would be enormous. One way or another, a carve-out for financial markets would have to be arranged.[63]

Thus I think that we should have an express carve-out for financial services, and two exceptions to the duty to disclose stated in more general terms. There should be no duty to disclose information (1) when the mistaken party was, or should be treated as, taking the risk that it might not have full or correct information; or (2) if it would be compatible with good faith and fair dealing to withhold it. We could then list the factors that the court should consider in deciding what was required by good faith and fair dealing. The list in the DCFR reads:

(a) whether the party had special expertise;
(b) the cost to the party of acquiring the relevant information;
(c) whether the other party could reasonably acquire the information by other means; and
(d) the apparent importance of the information to the other party.[64]

To this we might add (1) whether the information was likely to become public knowledge in any event and (2) whether it was information that would enable a party possessing it to make a better use of the relevant resources.

---

efficiently. Instead, it achieved an economic rent extraction made possible by the opacity of margins, the asymmetry of information and knowledge between end users of financial services and producers, and the structure of principal/agent relationships between investors and companies and between companies and individual employees.'

[63] Compare the Law Commissions' Report on *Unfair Terms in Contracts* (Law Com No 292, Scot Law Com No 199, 2005), draft Bill cl 29(4) and Explanatory Note 83.

[64] DCFR art II.-7:205(3).

REMEDIES

A party who has entered a contract under a mistake under the conditions set out above, and who does not fall within the carve-outs or the exceptions where disclosure should not be required, should have the right to avoid the contract. Avoidance seems the appropriate remedy, since one of the conditions is that, had he known the truth, he would not have entered the contract at all or would only have done so on fundamentally different terms. In the systems that recognize broad doctrines of mistake or fraud by silence, avoidance is the classic remedy.[65]

We saw that French and German law have recognized that D may have a duty to disclose facts in some circumstances even when D is now aware that C is in fact mistaken, and that breach of this duty gives rise to a claim for damages.[66] In principle, damages in German law will be on the reliance measure.[67] The PECL similarly allow a party who is entitled to avoid a contract for mistake also to recover damages if the other party knew or ought to have known of the mistake.[68] Giving a right to damages provides additional flexibility when the avoiding party chooses not to avoid the contract or has lost the right to do so,[69] but the

---

[65] The contract should be treated as voidable, not void. This will avoid difficulties over property questions arising when an apparent contract is void. See the discussion in J Cartwright, 'Defects of Consent in Contract Law', in A Hartkamp et al (eds), *Towards a European Civil Code* (4th edn, Kluwer, Alphen aan den Rijn, 2011), 537, 541–542.

[66] Above, pp 47 and 56.

[67] Ius Commune casebook, 527. French law does not recognize the different measures of damages, leaving the measure to the court.

[68] PECL art 4:117. The damages are to 'put the avoiding party as nearly as possible into the same position as if it had not concluded the contract', i.e. the damages are on the reliance measure.

[69] See PECL art 4:117(2), which limits the damages to 'the loss caused to it by the mistake...'. This was intended to prevent a party who does not avoid a contract which has turned out to be disastrous for other reasons from shifting the loss from the contract as a whole onto the other party (compare *William Sindall plc v Cambridgeshire CC* [1994] 1 WLR 1016, CA): see art 4:117 Comment C.

damages should not be limited to such cases. Given that we are providing a remedy only when D was in some sense at fault, I think that C should be entitled to damages for his reliance loss even if he does not avoid the contract.

The PECL, like a number of systems,[70] also give the court a power to adjust contracts which have been entered into as the result of a mistake.

Article 4:105: Adaptation of Contract

    (1) If a party is entitled to avoid the contract for mistake but the other party indicates that it is willing to perform, or actually does perform, the contract as it was understood by the party entitled to avoid it, the contract is to be treated as if it had been concluded as that party understood it. The other party must indicate its willingness to perform, or render such performance, promptly after being informed of the manner in which the party entitled to avoid it understood the contract and before that party acts in reliance on any notice of avoidance.

    (2) After such indication or performance the right to avoid is lost and any earlier notice of avoidance is ineffective.

    (3) Where both parties have made the same mistake, the court may at the request of either party bring the contract into accordance with what might reasonably have been agreed had the mistake not occurred.

A power to adapt the contract on these lines seems aimed primarily at mistakes over the terms of the contract. It is harder to see how it can be applied to cases in which one party was mistaken about the subject-matter or the circumstances surrounding the contract, as the facts are not normally capable of adjustment. It might be useful where one party has based its offer on a 'calculation error' such as

---

[70] See the notes to the DCFR version, DCFR art II.-7:203.

omitting to include the cost of one item of work; if the other party offered to pay for the omitted item, the mistaken party could then be required to perform the rest of the contract. But in most cases the mistaken party is likely to perform willingly if the omitted item is paid for. I think we can manage without a power of adaptation in our scheme.

SHOULD THE RULES BE MANDATORY?

A final question is whether the parties should be free to agree that the new rules should not apply to their contract. It might well be argued that when D knows of C's mistake and says nothing, silence being contrary to good faith and fair dealing, D commits fraud; and remedies for fraud by a contracting party cannot be excluded or restricted.[71] However, given that there would inevitably be some uncertainty over when disclosure is required, parties might legitimately want to exclude the new rules. Provided they are both fully aware of what they are agreeing to and its implications, that seems justifiable. Therefore I would suggest that an exclusion of the new rules or a restriction of the remedies arising under them should be permitted provided that the exclusion or restriction is reasonable, as is the position for misrepresentation.[72]

---

[71] *S. Pearson & Son Ltd v Dublin Corp* [1907] AC 351; *HIH Casualty and General Insurance Ltd v Chase Manhattan Bank* [2003] UKHL 6, [2003] 2 Lloyd's Rep. 61 at [16], [76], [121]. This will include, in a case where there is a duty of disclosure, fraudulent non-disclosure: *HIH Casualty and General Insurance Ltd v Chase Manhattan Bank* [2003] UKHL 6, at [21], [72]. The question whether a party can exclude liability for fraud by its employee or agent was left open: [2003] UKHL 6 at [16], [76]–[82].
[72] Misrepresentation Act 1967, s 3.

A PROVISIONAL PROPOSAL

So, to use 'Law Commission-speak', my 'provisional proposal' would be along the following lines:

(1) A party may avoid a contract on the ground of a mistake of fact or law[73] if:

    (a) the party, but for the mistake, would only have concluded the contract on fundamentally different terms, or would not have concluded a contract at all, and

    (b) the other party knew of the first party's mistake and its importance but, contrary to good faith and fair dealing, caused the contract to be concluded by leaving the mistaken party in error

unless

    (i) the mistake was merely as to the value of the performance the mistaken party was to give or receive, or

    (ii) the risk of the mistake was assumed, or in the circumstances should be borne, by the mistaken party.

(2) A party who had the right to avoid under the provision in para 1 should also have a right to claim damages to put him into the position he would have been in had the mistake been pointed out.

---

[73] There is not space here to discuss mistake of law as a separate topic. It suffices to say that many systems now treat mistakes as to law in the same way as mistakes as to the facts: see the notes to DCFR art II.-7:201. In English law payments made under a mistake of law may be recovered (*Kleinwort Benson Ltd v Lincoln City Council* [1999] 2 AC 349) and a common mistake of law may in principle render a contract void (*Brennan v Bolt Burdon* [2004] EWCA Civ 1017, [2005] QB 303, though it did not have this result on the facts, which involved a settlement agreement). If avoidance is sometimes to be permitted for a unilateral mistake as to the facts, there seems no reason to refuse it when the mistake is one of law.

I think that this proposal, though less certain than the current law, would nonetheless be workable. Rules that are a great deal less certain are used in countries whose economies seem as successful as our own.

Then I would add the following 'Consultation questions':

(a) Should the same apply when the non-mistaken party did not have actual knowledge of the importance of the mistake to the mistaken party but should have known of it?

(b) Should the same apply when the non-mistaken party did not have actual knowledge of the fact that the first party was mistaken but should have known of it?

DO WE WANT TO ADOPT THIS KIND OF MODEL?

Law Commissioners have the advantage that they will hear a range of views before deciding what to recommend (or even the chance of leaving difficult decisions to a successor). I am not yet committed to my provisional proposal. My aim is to stimulate debate rather than to give answers. But it would not be fair to sit down without offering some sort of view. However, in order to answer my own question, I have found that I have to go outside relatively narrow questions about unilateral mistake as to the facts. I find myself asking, what kind of contract law do we want?

I have already discussed how my proposal would bring advantages to certain kinds of transaction and certain parties. It would probably of much less relevance to large deals than to small ones, and be of less benefit to large businesses than to SMEs and the parties to some 'private' contracts.

Do we want to change the law to offer greater protection, when that change would necessarily be at a cost? It would be at a cost of increased uncertainty, because we would have to apply general standards such as whether good faith required that the mistake should have been pointed out. Some will also argue that it would inhibit the freedom of individuals to maximize their own advantage.

The question of the 'kind of contract law' we want goes wider than just cases of mistake. The same question, and our answer, must apply to several other areas of contract law. To take an obvious example, very much the same question has to be asked about controls over the contents of contracts, especially over standard terms.

In Chapter 2 I explained the difficulty I have had in discovering the policies that underlie the provisions of the civil codes I have looked at. But it is clear that overall, both French and German law take a much less individualistic line than English law. Taking just German law, I would say that if we set aside the special rules for the protection of, for example, consumers and employees, and concentrate on the 'residual law', the English and German laws of contract remain in sharp contrast.

The clearest demonstration of this is the controls over standard form contracts, originally effected by the courts on the basis of § 242, the article on good faith, and later put into legislative form, first in the Act on Standard Terms of Business (AGBG) of 1976[74] and then in 2001 brought into §§ 305 ff. BGB.

We all know that one problem with contracts that are in a standard form is that parties—and particularly a party who signs a standard form contract prepared by the other party— may do so without knowing what is in the standard form, or at least without understanding its implications. This is often termed the problem of 'unfair surprise'. German law tackles this problem head-on. § 305c BGB provides:

(1) Provisions in standard business terms which in the circumstances, in particular in view of the outward appearance of the contract, are so unusual that the contractual partner of the user could not be expected to have reckoned with them, do not form part of the contract.

English law has similar rules that apply to standard terms on notices and tickets, and it is now established that the more unusual the clause, the clearer the notice must

---

[74] The *Gesetz zur Regelung des Rechts der Allgemeinen Geschäftsbedingungen.*

be—the 'red-hand rule'.[75] But despite some suggestions that the red-hand rule might be applied also to signed documents,[76] it still seems to be the case that if you have signed a document which appears to be a contract[77] and which contains the offending term, it forms part of the contract whether or not you read it or understood it.[78] However unusual, the clause may be challenged only under the legislation governing unfair terms.[79] In English law, the burden is placed squarely on the contracting party: read the contract documents before you sign, however difficult that may be in practice—and if you don't have time to do so, or the ability to work out what the contract means, tough.

German law also has far more control over the content of standard form contracts. The BGB gives the court powers to review standard terms not only in consumer contracts, but also in B2B contracts under § 307:

> Provisions in standard business terms are invalid if, contrary to the requirement of good faith, they place the contractual partner of the user at an unreasonable disadvantage ...

This applies to standard contract terms of all types.[80]

---

[75] *Interfoto Picture Library Ltd v Stiletto Visual Programmes Ltd* [1989] QB 433, CA.

[76] *Ocean Chemical Transport Inc v Exnor Craggs Ltd* [2000] 1 Lloyd's Rep. 446, 454; *Amiri Flight Authority v BAE Systems Plc* [2003] EWCA Civ 1447 at [14]–[16]. In contrast, see *HIH Casualty & General Insurance Ltd v New Hampshire Insurance Company Independent Insurance Company Ltd* [2001] EWCA Civ 735, [2001] 2 Lloyd's Rep. 161 at [209]; *Do-Buy 925 Ltd v National Westminster Bank plc* [2010] EWHC 2862 (QB) at [91] ('not an extreme case, nor one in which there is any reason to depart from the principle that a party should be bound by a contract he has signed').

[77] The signature rule seems not to apply if the signing party could not reasonably have expected the document to contain contractual terms: *Grogan v Robin Meredith Plant Hire*, The Times, 20 February 1996 (not bound by term on document that appeared to be merely time sheets recording hours worked).

[78] See *L'Estrange v Graucob Ltd* [1934] 2 KB 394 and other authorities cited in Chitty para 12–002, n 5.

[79] Unfair Contract Terms Act 1977; Unfair Terms in Consumer Contracts Regulations 1999 (SI 1999/2083).

[80] At first it may seem that there is not even an exemption for 'core terms' such as the definition of the main subject-matter or the price (not

In contrast, for B2B contracts, the controls over contract terms provided by our Unfair Contract Terms Act 1977 are confined, in effect, to various varieties of exclusion and limitation clause. Moreover, I suspect that many lawyers think of the controls over terms in B2B contracts as being aimed more at procedural fairness—at the prevention of unfair surprise—than at control over the substance of what was agreed when the parties both knew and understood what was in the contract. That approach is evident, for example, in the responses described in the Report of the Law Commission and Scottish Law Commission on Unfair Contract Terms of 2005,[81] and in the Commissions' recommendations.[82] In contrast, German lawyers tell me that they regard it is as self-evident that § 307 BGB is aimed at terms which are unfair in substance, since procedural fairness is ensured by § 305c.

The difference between the English and continental laws on mistake of fact and the duty to disclose information illustrates a similar difference in attitude. English law is quite generous in affording relief to a party whose mistake was caused by being given incorrect information by the other party, even if that was done in all innocence and without negligence.[83] It seems to recognize that a party who has been given incorrect information is likely to assume that it need investigate no further: hence it is no bar to rescission

all of which will be individually negotiated and therefore beyond the reach of these provisions of the BGB). However, so far as fairness in substance is concerned the provisions are aimed primarily at terms which deviate from the 'essential' provisions of the statutory regime (see § 307(2)), and § 307(3) BGB limits the application of §§ 307–309 to terms which depart from the default rules under the BGB or provisions that supplement them. The BGB does not lay down rules on the subject-matter or the price, so such questions are outside the scope of §§ 307–309.

[81] *Unfair Terms in Contracts* (above, n 63), paras 4.13–4.16.

[82] Ibid, esp. paras 5.16–5.21. Cl 14 of the draft Bill on Unfair Contract Terms, 'The "Fair and reasonable test"', seeks to distinguish between the 'transparency' of the term and its 'substance and effect'; the explanatory note to cl 14(4), which lists the factors relevant to 'substance and effect', puts particular emphasis on the knowledge and understanding of the party affected by the term.

[83] *Redgrave v Hurd* (1881) 20 ChD 1, CA.

that he was given the opportunity to check the facts but did not trouble to do so.[84] But where the mistake was not the result of incorrect information given by the other party, English law allows D to take full advantage of C's mistake.

Why are the approaches so different? There are many possible reasons. One is simply that the laws are derived from different historical traditions. I will not explore this here because I do not think it is relevant. It seems unlikely that a field of law of such economic importance as contract would adhere to a tradition for purely historical reasons if that tradition was thought to be outdated. Not only was German law reviewed when the BGB was passed but it was the subject of extensive proposals for reform before 2001. There have been a number of criticisms of the law of mistake[85] but, so far as I am aware, no proposals for major reform.[86] This suggests that German lawyers are not dissatisfied with the current law. But if we ask why we each seem content to keep our different laws the way they are, there is at least one explanation which I think I can and should address. This is the kind of case which each legal system regards as typical.[87]

In a common law system, it is inevitable that the law is conditioned by the types of contract case which are being heard in the courts—or at least in the superior courts whose decisions 'count' as precedents and are reported. It is evident that a very high proportion of leading contract cases involve high-value contracts (after all, low value contracts are not worth fighting over, unless you are a Mr Ruxley or a Mr Forsyth[88]). Typically they are contracts between parties who are legally sophisticated or who can afford to take legal

[84] Ibid. at 14.

[85] e.g. Kramer argues that it does not deal properly with 'calculation mistakes': Kramer, IECL, s 80.

[86] See above, p 60.

[87] Other possible reasons are explored in H Beale, 'Characteristics of Contract Laws and the European Optional Instrument' (forthcoming).

[88] See *Ruxley Electronics and Construction Ltd v Forsyth* [1996] AC 344, where the amount at stake seemed hardly to justify an appeal to the House of Lords.

advice if they need it—even if advice is expensive, the cost will be low relative to the value of the deal. Thus they or their lawyers are likely to make sure that the right questions are asked beforehand. Moreover, the contracts are frequently in highly competitive markets, where (at least to an outsider) out-witting the other party, rather than collaboration, is the name of the game and negotiation is likely to be of the adversarial, uncooperative kind envisaged by Lord Ackner in his speech in *Walford v Miles*.[89] In cases of this kind, I suspect that even a French or German court would be likely to conclude that each party was taking upon itself the risk of incomplete information and would also refuse a remedy.

An additional factor is that often the relevant market is volatile. This is an old story but one that is worth recalling. Just think how many of the leading contract and sale of goods cases seem to have been fought because the market has changed dramatically and the party who stands to lose as a result is desperately seeking a way to get out of the contract and thus shift the market risk back to the other party. This is a zero-sum game. Parties have an incentive to litigate rather than to reach a mutually beneficial arrangement.

Against this background it is not surprising to find the courts, like the House of Lords in *Bunge Corp v Tradax Export SA*,[90] preferring bright-line rules that at least seem to promise predictable outcomes. As Priest showed, if there is uncertainty as to what the legal answer is, litigation is more likely, since if the parties hold different views as to the outcome of the case they may well think it worth investing resources in litigation—one party in trying to escape, the other in trying to prevent that.[91] So it is understandable that the courts should be reluctant to adopt open-textured standards, or indeed to fill in more gaps in the parties'

---

[89] [1992] 2 AC 128, 138.

[90] [1981] 1 WLR 711.

[91] G Priest, 'Breach and Remedy for the Tender of Non-conforming Goods' (1978) 91 Harv LR 960.

agreement than is absolutely essential to make the contract work.

Nor is uncertainty in the ultimate outcome the only problem. As the Law Commissions were told when they consulted on unfair contract terms, it is not enough to point out that when the parties were sophisticated or well advised, a court is most unlikely to hold that the terms to which they have signed up are unfair or unreasonable. The problem is that arguments about the meaning of a flexible standard can be used as a delaying tactic.[92] A party who needs extra time in which to find the money to pay will seize the opportunity to raise points that cannot be dealt with on an application for summary judgment, even if ultimately the arguments will almost certainly be rejected.[93]

So the nature of what we think of as our 'typical' cases seems to lead to an overwhelming pressure for certainty and minimal intervention, which colours not only the relevant decisions but much of our 'residual law' of contract. In a very real sense, the cases you find in Lloyd's commercial law reports typify English contract law as it applies in B2B cases.

Nor is it just a matter of judicial decisions. The approach affects our legislation, or the lack of it, because it is often cases of this type that the legislator or Law Commissioners envisage—or are told very firmly by City lawyers and the Financial Markets Law Committee (FMLC) they must take into account, cases to which they must not bring any additional uncertainty by suggesting the adoption of flexible

[92] See The Law Commissions' Report (above, n 63), paras 4.13 and 4.27.

[93] For example, the lessee under a finance lease might have agreed that the lessor should not be responsible for defects in the leased goods. This may be perfectly reasonable if the goods are covered by a warranty given to the lessee by the manufacturer which supplied them to the lessor. However, if the lessee has difficulty in meeting the instalments as they fall due, it may seek to use a defect in the goods as an excuse for not paying the lessor, arguing that the lessor's disclaimer is invalid under the Unfair Contract Terms Act 1977, s 7(3).

standards.[94] It is not just the litigation lawyers who take this view. The transactions lawyers who are drafting deals are worried by anything which might lead to their carefully-crafted agreements being challenged.

The result is that, while overall—taking into account developments in, for example, consumer and employment law—writers like Collins may be right to argue that English contract law has undergone a transformation into a law that aims to encourage fairness and to promote the social market,[95] the 'residual' law that applies, often in untrammeled form, to B2B contracts remains stoutly individualistic when compared to many of its continental counterparts. By and large it still rests on the assumption that parties can and should look out for their own interests, not only when negotiating prices or when signing up to standard form contracts, but also when ensuring that they have adequate information. If you don't know, ask. If you didn't ask, don't complain.

I would venture further. Whereas French law has strong moral overtones,[96] and the Nordic Contracts Act, § 33 on mistake[97] was seen in some countries as aimed at making good business morality into a legally binding principle,[98] the classical English model that still informs our 'residual' contract law seems happy to accept that there may be a gap between what the law requires and what parties may expect of each other because of their interest in keeping the deal viable for both parties, of their social relationship or even

---

[94] See the account of the responses received to the consultation on extending fairness controls to more types of clause in B2B contracts: Law Commissions' Report, (above, n 63) paras 4.08–4.12.

[95] H Collins, *The Law of Contract* (4th edn, CUP, Cambridge, 2008), esp. ch 2.

[96] D Harris and D Tallon (eds), *Contract Law Today: Anglo-French Comparisons* (Clarendon Press, Oxford, 1989), 385–386.

[97] See above, p 66.

[98] See Wilhelmsson (above, p 64, n 167), 172. See also Hayhä, 'Liability for Information in Private Law' in T Wilhelmsson & S Hurri (eds), *From Dissonance to Sense: Welfare state expectations, privatisation and private law* (Ashgate, Aldershot, 1999) 301, 326 (a 'welfarist approach' that party has duty to disclose relevant facts).

because of general morality. Remember that in *Smith v Hughes*[99] Cockburn CJ said that it was not a question of what a man of scrupulous morality or nice honour would do under such circumstances, but of what the law requires. His words suggest that he was quite content that there should be a gap between the law and morality or 'commercial expectations'.

Any law of contract sets outer limits on the parties' behaviour towards one another. Within those limits, the law leaves parties reasonably free to do what they want. Certain types of behaviour are treated as unacceptable in almost every system—fraud and duress, for example. Indeed, we go further than just providing remedies for fraud and duress: we give relief when there has been innocent misrepresentation, we refuse to uphold penalty clauses, and so on. But English law sets those limits more widely than many other European laws, and provided the parties' behaviour remains within these rather broad boundaries it is reluctant to lay down how they should behave towards each other, either in the course of performance or during the period of negotiation. That is a matter for the parties to agree on. If they do not make an express agreement on the relevant issue, we seem much less willing than our continental neighbours to prescribe obligations for them. Conversely—and the two go hand in hand—if the parties do reach an express agreement on more restrictive limits on what each may do, we are much more reluctant to interfere with what has been agreed, even if the agreement takes the shape of a standard form contract drafted by one party and not necessarily understood, or even read, by the other.

Part of the story is that we still try to limit the issues and the quantity of material that the court has to take into account, so as to achieve closure more readily, even if that means that some facts—for example, that one party had every commercial reason to expect the other to behave in a certain way—will simply be excluded from consideration

---

[99] (1871) LR 6 QB 597, 604, quoted above, p 18.

unless the expectation was 'written into' the contract.[100] The parol evidence rule was an obvious example and, though the rule itself seems to have been fatally weakened in the second part of the last century,[101] and now amounts to no more than a presumption that the written document contains all the terms agreed,[102] more recently courts have at least insisted that merger clauses are effective to exclude oral terms.[103] The rule excluding evidence of pre-contractual negotiations from being considered for the purposes of interpretation, recently reaffirmed by the House of Lords,[104] is another.

There is also the question of 'comparative advantage', the idea that it is easier and better for the parties to fix their obligations in advance than it would be for the court to do so after the event.[105]

Of course it is not wholly one way. Even in the commercial sphere, there are counter-tendencies. The *Hong Kong Fir* case[106] seems an obvious attempt to prevent a party faced with an unprofitable contract from justifying terminating it for spurious reasons. *Williams v Roffey Bros & Nicholls*

---

[100] See H Collins, *Regulating Contracts* (OUP, Oxford, 1999), ch 7.

[101] By cases such as *J. Evans & Son (Portsmouth) Ltd v Andrea Merzario Ltd* [1976] 1 WLR 1078. The Law Commission was asked to consider abolition of the rule; it concluded that there was no rule left to abolish: Law Commission Report, *Law of Contract: The Parol Evidence Rule* (Law Com No 154, 1986).

[102] Treitel, para 6–014.

[103] *AXA Sun Life Services plc v Campbell Martin Ltd* [2011] EWCA Civ 133, [2011] 2 Lloyd's Rep. 1. Most of the cases have involved the effect of 'no reliance' clauses aimed at preventing liability for misrepresentation arising: e.g. *Peekay Intermark Ltd v Australia & New Zealand Banking Group Ltd* [2006] EWCA Civ 386, [2006] 2 Lloyd's Rep. 511 at [54]–[60]; *Springwell Navigation Corp v JP Morgan Chase Bank* [2010] EWCA Civ 1221, [2010] 2 CLC 705 at [169]. The reasoning seems equally applicable to merger clauses.

[104] *Chartbrook Ltd v Persimmon Homes Ltd* [2009] UKHL 38, [2009] 1 AC 1101.

[105] See e.g. A Schwartz and R Scott, 'Contract Theory and the Limits of Contract Law' (2003) 113 Yale LJ 541, 549.

[106] *Hong Kong Fir Shipping Co Ltd v Kawasaki Kisen Kaisha Ltd (The Hong Kong Fir)* [1962] 2 QB 26.

(Contractors) Ltd[107] is an example of bringing law closer into line with the economic realities. Moreover, judges take different views of how best to promote the market. I will simply remind you of the approach of the series of cases on interpretation that led ultimately to Lord Hoffmann's speech in the *Investors Compensation Scheme* case;[108] and of the same judge's speech in *The Achilleas*.[109] In the interpretation cases, Lord Wilberforce's decision that the factual matrix of a contract can be used to interpret it[110] may have led inexorably to Lord Hoffmann's statement that anything[111] that was available to the parties and that is relevant may be considered.[112] However, it was Lord Hoffmann who made it clear that we are not concerned with some literal meaning of the words in a contract, it is always a question of how they would reasonably be understood in the context in which they were used.[113] It may be that this is only a shift from a more or less literal approach to a more purposive one;[114] but the net effect is that the court will have to spend more time and effort to determine the meaning of the contract than if it could apply a 'standard meaning' except where that would lead to an ambiguity or obvious nonsense. In *The Achilleas*[115] Lord Hoffmann held that the victim of a breach of contract cannot recover damages for a loss just because it was sufficiently likely— 'not unlikely'—to occur if the contract was broken. Even a

[107] [1991] 1 QB 1.

[108] *Investors Compensation Scheme Ltd v West Bromwich Building Society* [1998] 1 WLR 896.

[109] *Transfield Shipping Inc v Mercator Shipping Inc (The Achilleas)* [2008] UKHL 48, [2009] 1 AC 61.

[110] See *Prenn v Simmonds* [1971] 1 WLR 1381.

[111] Other than what was said in pre-contractual negotiations: *Chartbrook Ltd v Persimmon Homes Ltd* [2009] UKHL 38, [2009] 1 AC 1101.

[112] [1988] 1 WLR 896, 912–13, as qualified by what he said later in *Bank of Credit and Commerce International SA v Ali* [2001] UKHL 8, [2002] 1 AC 251 at [39].

[113] [1998] 1 WLR 896, 913; see also *Mannai Investment Co Ltd v Eagle Star Life Assurance Co Ltd* [1997] AC 749.

[114] Treitel para 6–011.

[115] *Transfield Shipping Inc v Mercator Shipping Inc (The Achilleas)* [2008] UKHL 48, [2009] 1 AC 61.

'not unlikely' loss is not recoverable if, in the circumstances in which the contract was made, it was not reasonable to think that the party who had broken the contract was assuming responsibility for a loss of the relevant kind. Some academics, myself included,[116] reacted strongly against this. At least on my part, this was because I had understood the case of *The Heron II* to adopt the opposite policy: if loss is a likely one, but a party does not wish to be liable for it should he break the contract, it is up to him to get an exclusion clause in the contract. The parties should fix the limits of liability in advance, rather than the court doing so after the event using a necessarily vague test such as 'assumption of responsibility'.

Nor should the differences be exaggerated. As Lord Hoffmann's speech made clear, the approach to the interpretation of contracts in English law is certainly not on the textual model advocated for B2B contracts by 'neoformalist' writers in the US like Alan Schwartz and Robert Scott, who would limit the court to considering 'the parties' contract, a narrative concerning whether the parties performed the obligations that the contract appears to require, [and] a standard English language dictionary....'.[117] Nor does English law take their line that the law should not provide either default rules (which are unlikely to meet the particularities of the case) nor broad standards such as whether goods are merchantable or performance is impracticable (which Schwartz and Scott say 'founder over the parties' need for ex ante guidance and the property of standards to create moral hazard'[118]), but to leave it to the parties to specify what they want.[119] English law does fill in

---

[116] See *Chitty*, para 26–100G.

[117] Schwartz & Scott (above, n 105), at 572; and see the discussion in their reply to their critics, 'Contract Interpretation Redux' (2010) 119 Yale LJ 926, 933.

[118] Schwartz & Scott (above, n 105), at 608.

[119] The consequences if the parties have not agreed on some point which turns out to be important are not developed at length in the article; the writers say little: 'What, then, is the proper role of courts in resolving disputes over incomplete contracts? It is appropriate for courts to apply a

many gaps in the parties' agreement, particularly when
parties have clearly not thought about some unlikely con-
tingency. But even then our law rather applies rules that,
compared to their continental counterparts, can seem simple if not crude. If the contract becomes permanently
impossible, the parties are discharged; likewise if there is
an unavoidable delay which is so serious that it frustrates
the purpose of the contract,[120] or if performing after the
delay is likely to be so different that it can be treated as
outside what was undertaken.[121] In contrast, where the
delay will not have such severe consequences, the general
rule is that a party must perform on time or be liable even if
it is impossible for him to do so. Commercially it would
be unreasonable to expect him still to perform, and many
different types of contract provide expressly that the party
delayed shall have an extension of time,[122] or will not be
liable for delays caused by force majeure.[123] Why, then, do
we still have the basic rule that the party who is delayed
by matters outside his control is liable? It seems to be what
economists have termed a 'penalty default' rule:[124] it is
not intended to provide the right solution itself but to
give a solution that is so unattractive that it will encourage

default standard as long as that standard does not create moral hazard.
Otherwise, courts have a choice: to dismiss a case on the ground that a
contract is too indefinite to enforce, or to read the contract to reach a
reasonable result.' (ibid, 608–609.) It might be thought that the rules and
standards applied by the law are a way of reaching a reasonable result.

[120] *Jackson v Union Marine Insurance Co* (1874) LR 10 CP 125.

[121] *Metropolitan Water Board v Dick, Kerr & Co* [1918] AC 119.

[122] This is the mechanism usually employed in building and engineering contracts. The clauses have a dual function: to prevent the contractor
being liable for late performance and also, when the delay has been
caused by the employer (for example by ordering extra work), to prevent
time becoming 'at large' and the employer losing the right to liquidated
damages even for delays for which the contractor was responsible. For a
succinct explanation, see Chitty, paras 37–115–37–118.

[123] On force majeure clauses see e.g. Chitty, paras 14–137 *et seq*;
E McKendrick, *Force Majeure and Frustration of Contract* (2nd edn, Lloyd's
of London Press, London, 1995); G Treitel, *Frustration and Force Majeure*
(2nd edn, Sweet & Maxwell, London, 2004).

[124] See I Ayres and R Gertner, 'Filling Gaps in Incomplete Contracts:
an Economic Theory of Default Rules' (1989) 99 Yale LJ 87.

the parties to devise a force majeure clause. They are in a better position to work out ex ante which delays should be covered and in what circumstances than the court will be to do it ex post.

So the English vision of contract law, or at least of this residual law that applies to B2B contracts and many private, non-business agreements, is often not a moral one, nor one which tries consistently to bring law into line with the parties' commercial expectations of what each other will or will not do. This is a law that gives strong ideological messages: look out for yourself, don't expect the court to come to the rescue. On a practical level, we want parties to deal with these problems for themselves. If they do, we will uphold what they have agreed. If they failed to do so, well, they will know for next time. Despite the counter-tendencies I have mentioned, I maintain my thesis that, on the whole, English 'residual contract law' recognizes that there is a gap between law and commercial expectations and, rather than try to bridge this gap, it leaves parties to do so themselves by the express terms; or, in our case, rather than require the disclosure of information according to a general standard such as good faith and fair dealing, it leaves the parties to safeguard themselves by making careful pre-contract enquiries.

There is some evidence, even, that this reflects the attitude of business people. We know that in some business relations, contract law is very much in the background.[125] It not the law but the economic pressure to do business in the future (and in order to do that, to maintain the firm's commercial relationships and its reputation in the market), and sometimes the social relations between the parties, which provide the immediate incentives to perform.[126] When a problem arises, it is those realities rather than formal contract law which tend to dictate the outcome—so

[125] H Beale and A Dugdale, 'Contracts between Businessmen: Planning and the Use of Contractual Remedies' (1975) 2 British Journal of Law & Society 45.

[126] See H Collins, *Regulating Contracts* (OUP, Oxford,1999), ch 6.

some sort of deal which enables the parties to continue trading is much more likely than a solution along the lines of the strict legal position. This does not mean that the law is completely irrelevant: as one manager put it, 'it is the umbrella under which we operate',[127] and when need be it would be resorted to (most obviously when a contracting party had failed to pay and there was little likelihood of future business from them[128]). But the businesspeople interviewed seemed to accept the gap between the law and the 'commercial reality'.

Indeed, there is some evidence that they regarded law and commercial trust as antithetical. Citing contract terms was thought to show that you didn't trust the other party, and was something that you just don't do if you want to go on doing business with the other party or to preserve your reputation.[129] (There are interesting suggestions that in this German attitudes are very different: some German contractors apparently see referring to the contract as a way of developing trust.[130])

We should not over-emphasize the extent to which business people 'do not rely on' contract law. Firstly, there may be great differences between sectors. The firms studied were engineering manufacturers of various kinds; and they seemed to form relatively closely-knit groups, in which 'reputational effects' are likely to be very strong.[131] But even in some markets in which one might expect firms' reputations to be known, such as the commodity and charter markets, the number of court cases suggest that in those sectors the parties may have a different attitude towards the law—they seem to litigate more readily, and they do not appear to regard litigation as fatal to

---

[127] Beale and Dugdale (above, n 125) at 48.

[128] Ibid, at 51.

[129] Ibid, at 47 and Collins (above, n 126) ch 5.

[130] See S Deakin, C Lane and F Wilkinson, 'Contract Law, Trust Relations and Incentives for Co-operation: a Comparative Study' in S Deakin and J Michie (eds), *Contracts, Co-operation and Competition* (OUP, Oxford, 1997), 105, esp. at 125–130.

[131] See Schwartz and Scott (above n 105), at 557.

commercial relationships. Secondly, the position is not static. Some years ago I used to lecture regularly to civil engineers. I was told that civil engineering contracts used also to be run on the basis of shared understandings between the engineer supervising the project for the employer and the contractor's representative (also an engineer) of what claims would be allowed and which would not; the contract remained in the bottom drawer. However, this had all changed. One reason was that in an era of greater accountability (the projects were mainly paid for from public funds), accountants were brought in and they insisted that payments be made 'by the book'. Another reason was that new forms of contract had come into use in which the roles were being re-assigned—such as design and build or management-only contracts—and when the parties are using a new and unfamiliar arrangement, the written contract is more clearly a specification of what each party should do and should expect of the other. But despite these qualifications to the non-use of contracts, I suspect there are many contracts where, to borrow Stewart Macaulay's phrase,[132] the gap between the 'paper deal' (the contract and its formal interpretation) and the 'real deal' persists.

There have been many calls to close the gap or, as Collins puts it, to bring the legal position closer to the expectations deriving from the economic realities and the social relationships between the parties.[133] Collins argues that the need

---

[132] See S Macaulay, 'The Real Deal and the Paper Deal: Empirical Pictures of Relationships, Complexity and the Urge for Simple, Transparent Rules' (2003) 66 MLR 44. Compare C Mitchell, "Contracts and Contract Law: Challenging the Distinction between the 'Real' and 'Paper' Deal" (2009) 29 OJLS 675.

[133] H Collins, *Regulating Contracts* (above n 126), 176. In contrast, Bernstein has studied customs and practices in a number of industries in the USA. She has concluded that, in many cases, it would be very difficult to incorporate trade understandings into contracts because there is little agreement on what the customs actually are: in particular, many terms and practices are understood differently in different parts of the country. She argues that these 'weak' customs do play an important role in commercial relationships, as what she terms 'relationship-preserving

for this is shown by the frequent use of arbitration.[134] Arbitrators do not have to apply the strict law; they can apply standards that reflect commercial realities. I am not sure how persuasive this argument is. First, the parties may choose arbitration for other reasons, such as the arbitrator's expert knowledge of the technical background or the confidentiality of arbitration. Secondly, not all arbitrators apply less strict rules. Scott argues that in the US arbitration is often chosen just because parties want a 'bright line' approach.[135] But both Collins and Scott may be correct if in each jurisdiction parties opt for arbitration in order to get something they will not get from the courts in the relevant jurisdiction.

However, if parties to the kinds of case English law treats as 'typical' did want this sort of rapprochement, I would expect there to have been more calls for it from practising lawyers. Rather in responses to consultations by the Law Commissions on controls over unfair terms—which might bring the paper deal and the real deal a little closer together—the dominant voices continue to say, 'hands off'. I am sure the reason is that for this type of case, it is thought to be a good thing for the gap to remain. It is better for parties to plan their own relationship than to have a judge fix it later.[136]

---

norms': seeing whether a new contracting partner will adhere to them is a useful way of establishing whether the partner is reliable. However, she argues that when the relationship breaks down—'end-game disputes'—the parties do not want any dispute to be decided by these customs but rather by the letter of the contract. See L Bernstein, 'The Questionable Empirical Basis of Article 2's Incorporations Strategy' (1996) 66 U of Chicago LR 710, and 'Private Commercial Law in the Cotton Industry: Creating Cooperation through Rules, Norms and Institutions' (2001) 99 Mich LR 1724.

[134] H Collins, *Regulating Contracts* (above n 126), 182.

[135] R Scott, 'The Death of Contract Law' (2004) 54 U of Toronto LJ 369, 378.

[136] It is of course very difficult for the parties to plan fully for long-term relationships. One puzzle is that in the US there have been a number of notorious cases involving long-term contracts where the initial arrangements have in some sense failed and the courts have attempted an adjustment: see Macaulay, above, n 132, 67 *et seq*. It is my impression

We find evidence of the reluctance to allow judicial 'interference' in B2B contracts in the provisions of the Unfair Contract Terms Act 1977. Our courts handle many cases that have no real connection with England save that the parties have chosen that the contract should be governed by English law. This is often coupled with a choice of England and Wales as the jurisdiction. This 'law for export' has deliberately been kept even closer to the classical model than the law for domestic consumption. Section 26 of the Act provides that it does not apply to international supply contracts, and section 27 that it does not apply to any contract that is only subject to English law because the parties have chosen that law. In proposing this exception from what was to become the 1977 Act, the Law Commissions argued simply:

> The effect of imposing our proposed controls in relation to those contracts might well be to discourage foreign businessmen from agreeing to arbitrate their disputes in England.[137]

Rightly or wrongly, it is clearly thought that minimal controls are what at least bigger business wants.

A superficial comparison of the cases that I have described as typical for the English courts with the cases that seem to appear in the French courts particularly—or at least those that are put forward by French colleagues for inclusion in comparative works—the average run seems very different. My impression is that cases in the French *tribunaux de commerce*[138] far more often involve small businesses, and do not involve contracts from highly volatile markets. Possibly this is because litigation is cheaper, possibly because French firms are less important in the markets

---

that we do not have much litigation on similar contracts in England. If that is correct, what is the explanation? And it is possible that my description of the 'typical' contract envisaged by English law should include 'relatively short-term'.

[137] LC 69 (1975) para 232.

[138] For the distinction between civil and commercial law in France see J Bell, S Boyron, S Whittaker, A Bell, M Freedland, and H Stalford, *Principles of French Law* (2nd edn, OUP, Oxford, 2008) ch 11.

that provide English courts with so much work, possibly even because French parties in volatile markets actually choose some other law to govern their contract. There is an old French jibe about English law being a law for shop-keepers[139]—fair enough. The standard response is to say that French law is a law for peasants. The response is meant in jest, and again we must not exaggerate differences—but there is a grain of truth in it. The typical cases which each law has to be fit to deal with in court seem to differ.

Though the Law Commissions thought that their propo-sals on exemption clauses were unsuitable for the export market, they obviously considered that they were suitable for domestic cases. In the same way, we might accept that our current rules on other types of standard contract term are suitable for the large commercial cases which are typical of the diet of our higher courts, but ask whether they are appropriate for all the types of contract to which they cur-rently apply. The Law Commissions have suggested they are not. The Law Commissions' Report on *Unfair Terms in Contracts*[140] recommended that controls over unfair terms in general, which presently apply only to consumer con-tracts,[141] should be extended also to small business con-tracts (a small business being those with no more than nine employees). The Report was accepted in principle by Government, though it has not yet been implemented.[142]

The rules of mistake and non-disclosure raise similar issues. The current 'residual regime' may well be suitable for the cases we typically see litigated and the kinds of transaction on which City lawyers spend most of their time. Even the limited proposal for change that I have made would lead to more issues having to be

---

[139] Presumably derived from Napoleon's jibe that 'L'Angleterre est une nation de boutiquiers'. Possible sources of the phrase are discussed in Wikipedia.

[140] See above, n 63.

[141] Unfair Terms in Consumer Contracts Regulations 1999 (SI 1999/2083).

[142] <http://www.justice.gov.uk/lawcommission/areas/unfair-terms-in-contracts.htm>.

investigated—what did C know or not know, and what did D know about C's position?—and increased uncertainty, in particular over what mistakes were sufficiently serious that they should have been pointed out and when good faith and fair dealing would permit non-disclosure. For the 'typical case', in which the parties are advised and can in any event bear a fair degree of risk, the change I have suggested may not be justified. But the current law may not be suitable for everyone. Not all small businesses are sufficiently sophisticated to know what questions to ask, or can afford to take appropriate advice. It is widely acknowledged that small businesses acting without legal advice are likely to be in a very different position from larger businesses which have it.[143] Thus Schwartz and Scott limit their proposals for a formalist approach to contract interpretation to cases involving corporations with more than five employees;[144] while conversely Stewart Macaulay says that he would be happier with Scott's approach 'if it were limited to cases where bargainers were represented by lawyers and the language of the writing was subject to negotiation'[145]—conditions which fit our 'typical cases'. The same may be true in consumer contracts, for the odd case in which the business does not seem obliged already to point out disadvantageous information,[146] and in contracts where neither party is a business. I have already outlined more than once the type of fact situation in which I think the change would make a real difference. So my argument is that for some sectors, the rule on mistake and non-disclosure should be changed.

---

[143] The many differences are explored in Garvin, 'Small Business and the False Dichotomies of Contract Law' (2005) Wake Forest LR 295.

[144] They would also apply to limited liability partnerships and professional partnerships of lawyers, accountants and the like, 'all of whom can be expected to understand how to make business contracts': Schwartz & Scott (above, note 105), 545.

[145] Macanlay (above, n 132), 51.

[146] Such as the sale of a new car which is about to be superseded by a new model, above, p 26.

One possibility is simply to change the residual rule of English law by legislation which would apply only in certain sectors—small business or SME contracts and non-business contracts, for example. However, we would then encounter the difficulty that any limit will be arbitrary and either over- or under-inclusive. I do not think, for example, that it would suffice to confine the rule to corporations that have fewer than five employees, nor to the class of small business contracts recommended in the Law Commissions' Report on Unfair Contract Terms.[147] Slips in calculation can occur in any size of business and I suspect that many businesses that are larger than these would still be hard-pushed to bear the risks that are sometimes created by evident errors in calculation.[148] I suspect the danger that parties enter contracts with inadequate information on matters which the other party knows about also occur just as much with SMEs as very small businesses.

The difficulties of targeting the reform accurately are such that many people, even if they are sympathetic to the call for reform, may conclude that it would be so difficult that it is simply not worth the candle.

But I think something needs to be done, to deal with at least the cases which involve an obvious abuse—the 'known mistake' cases—where the parties are not sophisticated and are not in an obviously competitive game. Moreover, I think it is likely that many smaller businesses would prefer a regime under which the other party would normally be unable to enforce a contract if it should have known that the small business had made a serious mistake. So I have come round to an alternative solution: we should allow the parties to choose the level of protection that

---

[147] See *Unfair Terms in Contracts* (above, n 63), paras 5.32–5.40 (inter alia, a limit of nine employees).

[148] The criteria of fewer than 250 employees and an annual turnover of less than EUR 50m used in the definition of SME in the proposed Regulation on a Common European Sales Law (see above, p 8), art 7(2), seems high but is perhaps nearer the mark. The figures are adopted from Commission Recommendation 2003/361 of 6 May 2003, see Recital 21 of the proposed CESL.

they want. It goes back to the idea of allowing parties to choose what law should govern their contract. English parties—particularly SMEs—are hardly likely to want to choose French or German law. They will want something with original texts in a language they can understand. An Optional Instrument could provide that.

The chief argument for an Optional Instrument like the proposed Common European Sales Law (CESL)[149] is that it would be useful to have a system for cross-border contracts, a system that all parties can become familiar with rather than having to learn about the law of every country with which they might do business,[150] and a system for which the original texts at least are available in many languages. But an Optional Instrument can have another advantage. Its rules can be geared to the needs of the parties who may want to use it. This is the case with the proposed CESL. For consumers, the CESL provides a high level of consumer protection, irrespective of who the business is. But for B2B contracts the purpose is to assist SMEs;[151] and looking at the substance of the proposed CESL, it seems to be specifically geared towards the needs of SMEs.[152] Thus there are provisions requiring disclosure,[153] controls over unfair terms,[154] and even a general provision on good faith and fair dealing,[155] all applicable to B2B contracts. If the CESL were to be adopted in its present form, for B2B contracts the parties would be free to choose the degree of freedom, the level of

---

[149] See above, p 8.

[150] See the Explanatory Memorandum to the proposed CESL, 3, and Recital 10.

[151] See Recital 2. Indeed the CESL will only apply to a B2B contract where one party is an SME, art 7(1); but Member States may make the CESL available for contracts between businesses of any size, art 13(b), see below, text at n 157.

[152] Certainly much of the discussion in the Expert Group which drafted the Feasibility Study (see above, p 8) was about what was needed by SMEs, and most of the relevant provisions have survived into the Commission's proposal.

[153] CESL arts 23 (Duty to disclose information about goods and related services), and 48 (Mistake) and 49 (fraud)—both along the lines of PECL.

[154] Art 86 (Meaning of 'unfair' in contracts between traders).

[155] Art 2.

legal risk, they want. If a party wants the comfort of protection against unfair terms and against the other party taking knowing advantage of their mistakes or their ignorance, they could seek to subject their contract to the CESL.[156]

Why limit this choice to cross-border contracts? Why not allow the parties to any B2B contract the possibility to choose between models, so they can seek greater protection if they want it? In this country we put great emphasis on freedom of choice. Why should we not allow the choice of the CESL or perhaps in the future a broader Optional Instrument, in place of a national domestic law, for contracting parties who are risk averse, who would prefer a law under which the other party has some responsibility to take their interest into account, and who want it in English? And indeed, the proposed Regulation on a CESL allows Member States to make the CESL available for domestic contracts between traders, and for contracts between traders of any size.[157]

There are, of course, difficulties. If the SME is not sufficiently sophisticated to ask the right questions in the first place, will it realize that it should try to have its contracts governed by the CESL? What if the other party prefers 'domestic' English law?

I think the answer to the first question is that it would not be hard to get across to small firms or indeed private individuals the notion that the new CESL is a new regime designed particularly for their use. They would not need to know the details, only that they should ask for the CESL to apply.[158]

---

[156] Leaving the parties to choose the level of protection seems more workable than adopting a general standard that should be applied differently in different markets, which was the suggestion of Wilhelmsson (above p 64, n 167).

[157] Proposed reg art 13.

[158] They may have to ask for it to apply in full, if the present text is maintained, as explained earlier (see above, p 10, n 44); art 8(3) of the proposed regulation seems to permit the parties to a B2B contract to choose only certain parts of the CESL to apply. This might result in an SME being misled into thinking that the CESL as a whole applies when in fact the other party's terms provide only for its partial application

As to the second question, of course the other party may not agree. If it finds that under the CESL, it may have to make disclosures it would not otherwise make, and that its terms, which under its 'domestic' national law would be immune, can be challenged as unfair, it will consider that it faces greater risks contracting under the CESL than under the domestic rules—a risk of greater liability if it is held not to have made adequate disclosure or if one of its terms is held to be invalid, and even if it is not, the risk of greater uncertainty and delay while the question is determined. The other party may therefore be unwilling to contract under the CESL without increasing the price at which it sells its goods or services, or decreasing the price at which it is willing to buy goods or services from the other. However, there are reasons to think that such a party, even if it is a large business, may sometimes be prepared to sign up to the CESL. The question will be whether the SME is prepared to 'pay the premium' in terms of increased prices when buying or decreased prices when selling. If SMEs prefer more freedom, possibly more certain outcomes but a higher risk if they make a mistake, they can stick with English law. It seems likely that SMEs are more risk averse than larger businesses; and it seems plausible that some SMEs will be prepared to pay a modest premium for greater legal protection. Indeed, it is not clear that only SMEs may want to use the CESL, for this or other reasons. Under the proposal, the CESL may only be used for B2B contracts if one of the parties is an SME,[159] though Member States may make the CESL available also when neither 'trader' (business) is an SME. It not obvious why choice of the CESL should be restricted to contracts involving an SME, even if it is doubtful whether it would often be chosen for contracts between larger entities.

(e.g. excluding the chapter on unfair terms). It would be better to provide that even in a B2B contract the choice must be all or nothing, as it is for B2C contracts.

[159] CESL Reg art 7(2).

So if we think that the existing law on mistake and non-disclosure is unfair and inefficient for at least some contracting parties, we have two ways forward. One is to amend English law, either in a targeted fashion or in general but with suitable 'carve-outs' for those who do not want the additional uncertainty that would be imposed. The other is to support the proposal for a CESL and, in future, the development of a broader Optional Instrument—one that, like the CESL, is specifically designed for parties who in general want a higher level of legal protection even at the price of some uncertainty, and for transactions for which the current highly individualistic English law is not best suited. Then we can leave English law as the contract law for the big fish. True, little fish may get in the pond by mistake or misjudgment, and then they may suffer. Perhaps if they fall prey to the worst forms of overreaching, the courts will still be able rescue them by developing the doctrine of unconscionability in the way seemingly contemplated by Lord Nicholls in the *BCCI* case.[160] But that is an issue to take up on another occasion.

[160] *Bank of Credit and Commerce International SA (In Liquidation) v Ali (No. 1)* [2001] UKHL 8, [2002] 1 AC 251, at [32]–[33]; see above, p 23.

Appendix
Extracts from principles,
legislation and reform proposals

PRINCIPLES OF EUROPEAN CONTRACT LAW

Article 1:101: *Application of the Principles*

(1) These Principles are intended to be applied as general rules of contract law in the European Union.

(2) These Principles will apply when the parties have agreed to incorporate them into their contract or that their contract is to be governed by them.

(3) These Principles may be applied when the parties:
   (a) have agreed that their contract is to be governed by 'general principles of law', the 'lex mercatoria' or the like; or
   (b) have not chosen any system or rules of law to govern their contract.

(4) These Principles may provide a solution to the issue raised where the system or rules of law applicable do not do so.

Article 4:103: *Fundamental Mistake as to Facts or Law*

(1) A party may avoid a contract for mistake of fact or law existing when the contract was concluded if:
   (a) (i) the mistake was caused by information given by the other party; or
       (ii) the other party knew or ought to have known of the mistake and it was contrary to good faith and fair dealing to leave the mistaken party in error; or
       (iii) the other party made the same mistake, and
   (b) the other party knew or ought to have known that the mistaken party, had it known the truth, would not have entered the contract or would have done so only on fundamentally different terms.

(2) However a party may not avoid the contract if:
   (a) in the circumstances its mistake was inexcusable, or
   (b) the risk of the mistake was assumed, or in the circumstances should be borne, by it.

Article 4:107: *Fraud*

(1) A party may avoid a contract when it has been led to conclude it by the other party's fraudulent representation, whether by words or conduct, or fraudulent nondisclosure of any information which in accordance with good faith and fair dealing it should have disclosed.

(2) A party's representation or non-disclosure is fraudulent if it was intended to deceive.

(3) In determining whether good faith and fair dealing required that a party disclose particular information, regard should be had to all the circumstances, including:
  (a) whether the party had special expertise;
  (b) the cost to it of acquiring the relevant information;
  (c) whether the other party could reasonably acquire the information for itself; and
  (d) the apparent importance of the information to the other party.

DRAFT COMMON FRAME OF REFERENCE

II.–7:201: Mistake

(1) A party may avoid a contract for mistake of fact or law existing when the contract was concluded if:
  (a) the party, but for the mistake, would not have concluded the contract or would have done so only on fundamentally different terms and the other party knew or could reasonably be expected to have known this; and
  (b) the other party;
    (i) caused the mistake;
    (ii) caused the contract to be concluded in mistake by leaving the mistaken party in error, contrary to good faith and fair dealing, when the other party knew or could reasonably be expected to have known of the mistake;
    (iii) caused the contract to be concluded in mistake by failing to comply with a pre-contractual information duty or a duty to make available a means of correcting input errors; or
    (iv) made the same mistake.

(2) However a party may not avoid the contract for mistake if:
  (a) the mistake was inexcusable in the circumstances; or
  (b) the risk of the mistake was assumed, or in the circumstances should be borne, by that party.

II.–7:203: Adaptation of contract in case of mistake

(1) If a party is entitled to avoid the contract for mistake but the other party performs, or indicates a willingness to perform, the obligations under the contract as it was understood by the party entitled to avoid it, the contract is treated as having been concluded as that party understood it. This applies only if the other party performs, or indicates a willingness to perform, without undue delay after being informed of the manner in which the party entitled to avoid it understood the contract and before that party acts in reliance on any notice of avoidance.

(2) After such performance or indication the right to avoid is lost and any earlier notice of avoidance is ineffective.

(3) Where both parties have made the same mistake, the court may at the request of either party bring the contract into accordance with what might reasonably have been agreed had the mistake not occurred.

II.–7:205: Fraud

(1) A party may avoid a contract when the other party has induced the conclusion of the contract by fraudulent misrepresentation, whether by words or conduct, or fraudulent non-disclosure of any information which good faith and fair dealing, or any pre-contractual information duty, required that party to disclose.

(2) A misrepresentation is fraudulent if it is made with knowledge or belief that the representation is false and is intended to induce the recipient to make a mistake. A non-disclosure is fraudulent if it is intended to induce the person from whom the information is withheld to make a mistake.

(3) In determining whether good faith and fair dealing required a party to disclose particular information, regard should be had to all the circumstances, including:

(a) whether the party had special expertise;

(b) the cost to the party of acquiring the relevant information;

(c) whether the other party could reasonably acquire the information by other means; and

(d) the apparent importance of the information to the other party.

UNIDROIT PRINCIPLES OF INTERNATIONAL COMMERCIAL CONTRACTS 2010

PREAMBLE

(Purpose of the Principles)

These Principles set forth general rules for international commercial contracts.

They shall be applied when the parties have agreed that their contract be governed by them.

They may be applied when the parties have agreed that their contract be governed by general principles of law, the *lex mercatoria* or the like.

They may be applied when the parties have not chosen any law to govern their contract.

They may be used to interpret or supplement international uniform law instruments.

They may be used to interpret or supplement domestic law.

They may serve as a model for national and international legislators.

ARTICLE 3.2.1

(Definition of mistake)

Mistake is an erroneous assumption relating to facts or to law existing when the contract was concluded.

ARTICLE 3.2.2

(Relevant mistake)

(1) A party may only avoid the contract for mistake if, when the contract was concluded, the mistake was of such importance that a reasonable person in the same situation as the party in error would only have concluded the contract on materially different terms or would not have concluded it at all if the true state of affairs had been known, and

    (a) the other party made the same mistake, or caused the mistake, or knew or ought to have known of the mistake and it was contrary to reasonable commercial standards of fair dealing to leave the mistaken party in error; or

    (b) the other party had not at the time of avoidance reasonably acted in reliance on the contract.

(2) However, a party may not avoid the contract if

    (a) it was grossly negligent in committing the mistake; or

    (b) the mistake relates to a matter in regard to which the risk of mistake was assumed or, having regard to the circumstances, should be borne by the mistaken party.

ARTICLE 3.2.5

(Fraud)

A party may avoid the contract when it has been led to conclude the contract by the other party's fraudulent representation, including language or practices, or fraudulent non-disclosure of circumstances which, according to reasonable commercial standards of fair dealing, the latter party should have disclosed.

PROPOSAL FOR A COMMON EUROPEAN SALES LAW

Article 48

Mistake

1. A party may avoid a contract for mistake of fact or law existing when the contract was concluded if:
    (a) the party, but for the mistake, would not have concluded the contract or would have done so only on fundamentally different contract terms and the other party knew or could be expected to have known this; and
    (b) the other party:
    (i) caused the mistake;
    (ii) caused the contract to be concluded in mistake by failing to comply with any pre-contractual information duty under Chapter 2, Sections 1 to 4;
    (iii) knew or could be expected to have known of the mistake and caused the contract to be concluded in mistake by not pointing out the relevant information, provided that good faith and fair dealing would have required a party aware of the mistake to point it out; or
    (iv) made the same mistake.
2. A party may not avoid a contract for mistake if the risk of the mistake was assumed, or in the circumstances should be borne, by that party.
3. An inaccuracy in the expression or transmission of a statement is treated as a mistake of the person who made or sent the statement.

Article 49

Fraud

1. A party may avoid a contract if the other party has induced the conclusion of the contract by fraudulent misrepresentation, whether by words or conduct, or fraudulent non-disclosure of any information which good faith and fair dealing, or any pre-contractual information duty, required that party to disclose.
2. Misrepresentation is fraudulent if it is made with knowledge or belief that the representation is false, or recklessly as to whether it is true or false, and is intended to induce the recipient to make a mistake. Non-disclosure is fraudulent if it is intended to induce the person from whom the information is withheld to make a mistake.
3. In determining whether good faith and fair dealing require a party to disclose particular information, regard should be had to all the circumstances, including:
    (a) whether the party had special expertise;
    (b) the cost to the party of acquiring the relevant information;
    (c) the ease with which the other party could have acquired the information by other means;
    (d) the nature of the information;
    (e) the apparent importance of the information to the other party; and
    (f) in contracts between traders good commercial practice in the situation concerned

NEW ZEALAND CONTRACTUAL MISTAKES ACT 1977

6 Relief may be granted where mistake by one party is known to opposing party or is common or mutual

(1) A Court may in the course of any proceedings or on application made for the purpose grant relief under section 7 of this Act to any party to a contract—
    (a) If in entering into that contract—
        (i) That party was influenced in his decision to enter into the contract by a mistake that was material to him, and the existence of the mistake was known to the other party or one or more of the other parties to the contract (not being a party or parties having substantially the same interest under the contract as the party seeking relief); or

   (ii) All the parties to the contract were influenced in their respective decisions to enter into the contract by the same mistake; or

   (iii) That party and at least one other party (not being a party having substantially the same interest under the contract as the party seeking relief) were each influenced in their respective decisions to enter into the contract by a different mistake about the same matter of fact or of law; and

(b) The mistake or mistakes, as the case may be, resulted at the time of the contract—

   (i) In a substantially unequal exchange of values; or

   (ii) In the conferment of a benefit, or in the imposition or inclusion of an obligation, which was, in all the circumstances, a benefit or obligation substantially disproportionate to the consideration therefor; and

(c) Where the contract expressly or by implication makes provision for the risk of mistakes, the party seeking relief or the party through or under whom relief is sought, as the case may require, is not obliged by a term of the contract to assume the risk that his belief about the matter in question might be mistaken.

FRENCH *CODE CIVIL*

Article 1109: There is no valid consent, where the consent was given only by error, or where it was extorted by duress or abused by deception.

Article 1110: Error is a ground for annulment of an agreement only where it rests on the very substance of the thing which is the object thereof.

   It is not a ground for annulment where it only rests on the person with whom one has the intention of contracting, unless regard to/for that person was the main cause of the agreement.

AVANT-PROJET CATALA[1]

Art 1110 If one of the parties knows or ought to have known information which he knows is of decisive importance for the other, he has an obligation to inform him of it.

---

[1] Translation from J Cartwright, S Vogenauer, and S Whittaker (eds), *Reforming the French Law of Obligations: Comparative Observations on the Avant-projet de réforme du droit des obligations et de la prescription* (Hart, Oxford, 2009), 639.

However, this obligation to inform exists only in favour of a person who was not in a position to inform himself, or who could legitimately have relied on the other contracting party, by reason (in particular) of the nature of the contract or the relative positions of the parties.

A party who claims the benefit of an obligation to inform has the burden of proving that the other party knew or ought to have known the information in question, but it is then for that other party to show that he has fulfilled his obligation in order to escape liability.

Information is relevant if it has a direct and necessary link with the subject-matter or the cause of the contract.

Art 1110–1 In the absence of an intention to deceive, a failure to fulfil an obligation to inform gives rise to liability in the party subject to it.

BGB

§ 119: *Voidability for mistake*

(1) A person who, when making a declaration of intent, was mistaken about its contents or had no intention whatsoever of making a declaration with this content, may avoid the declaration if it is to be assumed that he would not have made the declaration with knowledge of the factual position and with a sensible understanding of the case.

(2) A mistake about such characteristics of a person or a thing as are customarily regarded as essential is also regarded as a mistake about the content of the declaration.

§ 122: *Liability in damages of the person declaring avoidance*

(1) If a declaration of intent is void under section 118, or avoided under sections 119 and 120, the person declaring must, if the declaration was to be made to another person, pay damages to this person, or failing this to any third party, for the damage that the other or the third party suffers as a result of his relying on the validity of the declaration; but not in excess of the total amount of the interest which the other or the third party has in the validity of the declaration.

(2) A duty to pay damages does not arise if the injured person knew the reason for the voidness or the voidability or did not know it as a result of his negligence (ought to have known it).

BW

Article 6:228: 1. A contract which has been entered into under the influence of error and which would not have been entered into had there been a correct assessment of the facts, can be annulled:

a. if the error is imputable to information given by the other party, unless the other party could assume that the contract would have been entered into even without this information;
b. if the other party, in view of what he knew or ought to know regarding the error, should have informed the party in error;
c. if the other party in entering into the contract has based himself on the same incorrect assumption as the party in error, unless the other party, even if there had been a correct assessment of the facts, would not have had to understand that the party in error would therefore be prevented from entering into the contract.

2. The annulment cannot be based on an error as to an exclusively future fact or an error for which, given the nature of the contract, common opinion or the circumstances of the case, the party in error should remain accountable.

NORDIC CONTRACTS ACT

33. Even if a declaration of intention shall otherwise be regarded as valid, the person to whom the declaration was made may not, however, rely on the declaration if, as a result of circumstances existing at the time when he had notice of the declaration and of which he must be deemed to have known, it would be against the principles of good faith to enforce the declaration.

36. (1) A contract may be modified or set aside, in whole or in part, if it would be unreasonable or at variance with the principles of good faith to enforce it. The same applies to other juristic acts.

(2) In making a decision under subsection (1) hereof, regard shall be had to the circumstances existing at the time the contract was concluded, the terms of the contract and subsequent circumstances.

THE AUTHOR'S 'PROVISIONAL PROPOSAL'

(1) A party may avoid a contract on the ground of a mistake of fact or law if:

   (a) the party, but for the mistake, would only have concluded the contract on fundamentally different terms, or would not have concluded a contract at all, and

   (b) the other party knew of the first party's mistake and its importance but, contrary to good faith and fair dealing, caused the contract to be concluded by leaving the mistaken party in error

   unless

   (i) the mistake was merely as to the value of the performance the mistaken party was to give or receive or

   (ii) the risk of the mistake was assumed, or in the circumstances should be borne, by the mistaken party.

(2) A party who had the right to avoid under this provision should also have a right to claim damages to put him into the position he would have been in had the mistake been pointed out.

'CONSULTATION QUESTIONS':

Should the same apply when the non-mistaken party did not have actual knowledge of the importance of the mistake to the mistaken party but should have known of it?

Should the same apply when the non-mistaken party did not have actual knowledge of the fact that the first party was mistaken but should have known of it?

Index

**Academy of European Private
    Lawyers** 3
arbitration
    arbitration clauses 6
    arbitrators' expert
        knowledge 115
    bright line approach 115
    confidentiality 115
    dispute resolution 6
    forum shopping 115–16
Australia
    duty of disclosure 35
    mere silence 34–5
    misleading deceptive
        conduct 34
    misleading information 35
    misrepresentation 35
    unconscionability
        lack of explanation 36
        special disadvantage 36
    volunteering information 35
Avant-projet Catala 12, 45, 48,
    51–2, 131–2

business environment
    business to business (B2B)
        contracts 105–6, 110,
        112, 116
    commercial
        expectations 106–7, 112
    commercial reality 112–15
    commercial
        relationships 114
    commercial trust 113
    economic pressures 112

judicial interference 116
    paper deal/real deal
        gap 114–15
    reputational effects 113
    small businesses 119–22
**business to business (B2B)
    contracts**
    business environment
        105–6, 110, 112, 116
    Common European Sales
        Law (CESL) 9–10,
        120, 122
    default rules 6
    Optimal Instrument 8
    unfair contract terms 102,
        116
**business to consumer (B2C)
    contracts**
    Common European Sales
        Law (CESL) 9–10
    Optimal Instrument 9–10

Canada
    duty to disclose 36–7
    mistaken calculations
        37–9
    mistaken offers 37–9
    sale of property 37
    tenders 38–9
    unconscionability 36
**Common European Sales Law
    (CESL)**
    adoption 11
    advantages 120
    avoidance of contract 129

Common European Sales Law (CESL) *(cont.)*
business to business (B2B) contracts 9–10, 120, 122
business to consumer (B2C) contracts 9–10
comity principles 11
consumer protection 10, 120
contentious nature 11
cross-border contracts 9, 120
default rules 10
disclosure 120, 122
dispositive rules 9
European Court of Justice supervision 11
fair dealing 120
fraud 130
good faith 120
governing law 9
interpretation 11
legal protection 123
legal risk 121–2
mandatory rules 10–11
mistake 129
national law 9–11
operation 9
optional nature 9
proposal 8, 9, 11
small businesses 120–2
unfair contract terms 120–1
Common Frame of Reference (CFR)
see also **Optimal Instrument**
guide for legislators 6–8
Commonwealth laws
Australia 34–6
see also **Australia**
Canada 36–9
see also **Canada**
mistake
contracts not voidable 34

divergences 33
equitable intervention 33
New Zealand 39–41
see also **New Zealand**
Convention on the International Sales of Goods (CISG)
national law 9
relevant types of contract 9

demurrage
amount payable 1
binding settlement 2
mistake as to surrounding facts 1, 30
non-disclosure of facts 1
differences between English/ European laws
academic debate 13
alternative model 73
case for review 13, 14, 26
contracts of insurance 20
duty of disclosure 20–2, 29
see also **duty of disclosure**
duty to take reasonable care 21
extent of differences 12, 19–20
granting relief 73
historical traditions 103
Law Commission Programmes 13
misrepresentation 21
mistake as to facts 13–14
mistake caused by incorrect information 102
non-disclosure 13, 14
philosophical issues 14
policy issues 14
review of differences 73
sale of goods
goods fit for purpose 21, 26

goods of satisfactory
    quality 21, 26
implied terms 26
sale in course of business 26
sales of land
    caveat emptor 26, 28
    defective title 27
    indirect duty to
        disclose 26–7
    National Conveyancing
        Protocols 25, 27–8
    unusual facts (unknown
        unknowns) 27–8
disclosure of information
duty of disclosure *see* **duty
    of disclosure**
non-disclosure
    exploitation of another's
        ignorance 30
    increase in welfare 30
    justification 30
standardized
    procedures 24–6
**Draft Common Frame of
    Reference (DCFR)**
see also **Optimal Instrument**
adaptation of contract 126
avoidance of contract 87
duty to disclose 94
fraud 127
generally 3, 4
knowledge of mistake 87
mistake 126–7
mistake as to motive 87
mistake of fact 87
mistake of law 87
protected information 94
unilateral mistake 19
duty of disclosure
consumer's duty 20–21
contracts of insurance 20
direct duty

family arrangements 21
prospective business
    partners 21
relationships of trust and
    confidence 21, 29
statutory duties 21
suretyship 21
financial services
    contracts 24
indirect duty
    defects 21
    goods fit for purpose 21
    goods of satisfactory
        quality 21
    sales of land 26–7
    supply of services 22
long-standing
    relationships 29
relationships of trust and
    confidence 21, 29

English contract law
alternative model 73
business environment
    business to business (B2B)
        contracts 105–6, 110,
        112, 116
    commercial
        expectations 106–7,
        112
    commercial reality
        112–15
    commercial
        relationships 114
    commercial trust 113
    economic pressures 112
    judicial interference 116
    paper deal/real deal
        gap 114–15
    reputational effects 113
    small businesses 119–22
consumer cases 118

English contract law (*cont.*)
  differences with European
    laws *see* **differences
    between English/
    European laws**
  differing legal
    attitudes 113–14
  enforcement 77, 110–11
  exclusion clauses 102, 117
  fair dealing 112, 118
  force majeure clauses 112
  freedom of choice 121
  good faith 112, 118
  governing law 116
  individualistic nature 106
  informed consent
    model 71–2, 77–8
  legislation 105
  level of protection 119–120
  litigation 103–10
  see also **litigation**
  mistake *see* **mistake**
  models to avoid 76–7
  morality 107
  penalty default rule 111
  plausible informed consent
    model *see* **plausible
    informed consent
    model**
  price
    exchange at market
      price 77–8
    fairness of price 78
  promise
    non-binding promise 77
    performance of
      promises 77, 110–11
  residual contract law 105–6,
    112, 117, 119
  review 73, 75, 77, 118–19,
    123

  social relationships 106,
    112, 114
  unavoidable delay 111
  unbalanced contracts 78
  unconscionability 123
  unlikely contingencies 111
  unusual risks 75
EU law
  Directives 3
  European Court of Justice
    decisions 3
  harmonization 6–8
  revision 6
European Commission
  Action Plan for European
    Contract Law 6
  Green Paper on policy
    options 7
European Contract Code 3
European contract law
  acceptable principles
    4, 42
  Acquis Principles 3
  compromise principles
    4, 42
  Directives 3
  European Civil Code 7, 8
  European Commission
    Action Plan 6
  European Court of Justice
    decisions 3
  harmonization 6–8
  mistake
    autonomy of the will 42
    procedural fairness 42
    protection of informed
      consent 42
    reliance on contract 42
    substantive fairness 42
  shared principles
    4, 7, 42

Financial Services Authority (FSA)
Conduct of Business (COB) Rules 23
High Level Principles 24
financial services contracts
breach of statutory duty 24
duty of disclosure 24
see also **duty of disclosure**
fair treatment 24
informational requirements 24
investment businesses 23
regulation 23
France
acceptance of risk 45
annulment of contract 43–7, 131
Avant-projet Catala 12, 45, 48, 51–2, 131–2
avoidance of contract 46
Code civil 42–3, 45, 49, 131
consensual contracts 42–3
contract law
contractual solidarity 49–51
expressions of will 49
individual autonomy 49–52
litigation 116–17
networks of contracts 49–50
protection of reliance 72
relief for mistake 51
voluntarism 49
deception 131
deliberate silence 46–8, 51, 88
duress 131
duty of disclosure 50–1, 95
duty to inform 73
duty to warn 83
fraud cases 47–8

incorrect information 43
mistake
common mistake 43
inexcusable mistake 90
knowledge of mistake 46
mere mistake of motive 44–5, 47
misconduct requirement 46
mistake as to essential characteristic 44
mistake as to essential element 42–3
mistake as to subject-matter 43–6
mistake as to value 45, 51
mistake not inexcusable 72
mistake through own fault 46
relief for mistake 51
moral overtones 106
protection of informed consent 42
relative nullity 43
fraud
avoidance of contract 1
fraud by silence 47, 55, 57, 64, 73, 88–9
non-disclosure 1, 2

Germany
absence of relevant party 59
balancing of interests 59
Bürgerliches Gesetzbuch (BGB) 52–4, 56–7, 60, 72, 132
carelessness 55–6
consumer protection 100–1
contract law
avoidance of contract 72, 132

Germany (*cont.*)
  binding nature of
    contract 52
  breach of contract 53, 58
  protection of reliance 72
  damages 95, 132
  defective goods 54, 58
  deliberate silence 55–6
  dishonest non-disclosure 57
  duty to disclose 55–8, 60,
    89, 95
  duty to inform 57, 73
  duty to warn 83
  fraud 55, 57, 59, 89
  justifiable reliance 55
  law reform 103
  misrepresentation
    half-truth 59
    non-fraudulent
      misrepresentation 57
    positive
      misrepresentation 57
  mistake
    culpa in contrahendo 56–9
    errors as to value 54
    errors in declaration 52,
      59
    errors in motivation 52–3,
      59, 60
    knowledge of mistake 55
    minor mistakes 54
    mistake as to
      calculation 60
    mistake as to essential
      qualities 60
    mistake as to subject-
      matter 53–4
    unilateral mistake 55
  procedural fairness 102
  reliance loss 55, 59, 79
  sale of businesses 59
  social responsibility 59–60

standard form
  contracts 100–1
unfair contract terms 102
will theory 52

informed consent
  see also **plausible informed
    consent model**
  contract law 71–2, 77–8
insurance contracts
  duty of disclosure 20
  duty to take reasonable
    care 21

Lando Principles *see*
    **Principles of European
    Contract Law (PECL)**
Law Commission
  Conveyancing Standing
    Committee 28
  Ninth Programme of
    Work 13
  Tenth Programme of
    Work 13
  unfair contract terms 102,
    105, 117, 119
litigation
  adversarial nature 104
  breach of contract 109–10
  bright line rules 104
  certainty requirement 104–5
  comparative advantage 108
  competitive market
    environment 104
  high-value contracts 103–4
  interpretation cases 109–10,
    118
  limiting the issues 107
  merger clauses 108
  open-textured
    standards 104–6
  parole evidence rule 108

pre-contractual
negotiations 108
relevant market 104
unprofitable contracts 108

misrepresentation
innocent
misrepresentation 107
non-fraudulent 57
positive
misrepresentation 37,
89
rescission 16
mistake
acquiescence 15
avoidance of contract 16, 18
calculation mistake 37–9, 60,
75, 92, 96–7
common mistake 16–17
disadvantaged mistaken
party 75–6
exploiting another's
ignorance 30
facts not as assumed 15
incorrect belief 15
knowledge of mistake 2, 18
legal relevance 14–16
misrepresentation 16
mistake as to facts 1, 13
mistake as to terms 15, 18
mistake irrelevant 79
mistake not shared 15
mistaken belief 15
mistaken identity 16
mistaken offers 15
mutual
misunderstanding 15
nature of subject-matter 15
positive belief 15
pre-contract enquiries 2
rescission 16

reform 73, 75, 77, 118–19,
123
Roman law 44
surrounding facts 1, 15, 30
unconscionable
bargains 22–23
underlying
assumptions 1, 15
unilateral mistake 17–18
value of subject-matter 22
models for English law
consumer protection 100
exclusion of new rules 97
mandatory rules 97
plausible informed consent
model *see* **plausible
informed consent
model**
provisional proposal
advantages 99
avoidance of contract 98
consultative
questions 134
cost of change 99
fair dealing 98
good faith 98–9
increased protection 99
increased uncertainty 99
knowledge of mistake 98
mistake as to fact 98
mistake as to law 98
mistake as to value 98
mistake in error 98
no actual knowledge 99
right to damages 98
risk of mistake
assumed 98
should have known of
mistake 78, 82–4, 89,
90, 99
stimulating debate 99

models for English law (*cont.*)
remedies
adaptation of
contract 96–7
avoidance of contract 95
calculation errors 96–7
damages 95–6, 98
fraud 97
mistake as to terms 96
rescission 102
restriction 97
standard form contracts 100
standard terms 100

National Conveyancing Protocols
pre-contract enquiries 25
sales of land 27–8
Netherlands
contract law
annulment of contract 61
avoidance of
contract 61–2
contract influenced by
error 61
dishonest silence 63
Dutch Civil Code 61–2, 133
duty to inform 63
duty to warn 83
fraud 63
mistake
knowledge of
mistake 62–3
legal relevance 61
positive incorrect
belief 62
unilateral mistake 61–3
New Zealand
fairness of exchange 40–1,
72, 77
judicial discretion 40, 76
mistake

common mistake 40,
130–1
Contractual Mistakes
Act 130
disproportionate
benefit 40
knowledge of
mistake 39–40
mistake as to facts
mistake as to terms 39–41
risk of mistake 40
unequal exchange of
values 40
unilateral mistake 40
sales of land 41
unjust enrichment 41
Nordic laws
contract law
equality of exchange 67–8,
72
failure to perform 65
good faith 67–8, 76
non-conforming goods
(Denmark) 65
reliance on contract
66, 68
defective property
Norway 65
Sweden 65
disclosure of information
(Finland) 66
fraud 64
mistake
advantage taken of
promisor's
ignorance 66
damages for mistake 67
fault 67
knowledge of mistake
66–7
mistake in declaration 64
risk of mistake 67

Nordic Contracts Act 64, 66, 72, 76, 106, 133
procedural unfairness 67, 72
substantive unfairness 67, 72

Optional Instrument
adoption 14
advantages 120
business to business (B2B) contracts 8
business to consumer (B2C) contracts 8
cross-border contracts 8, 120
development 2, 7–8, 11, 123
Expert Group 8
governing contracts 2
legal base 11
related services 8

plausible informed consent model
actual knowledge of mistake 79, 81–2, 89
avoidance of contract 84
binding force of contract 84
causation 85, 90
contract price 87
contributory negligence 90
deliberate non-disclosure 89
fair dealing 93–4
fraud by silence 88–9
fundamental mistake 84–5, 89
good faith 93–4
importance of subject-matter 89
importance sufficiently apparent 85
information enabling better use of resources 94
judicial discretion 84

knowledge of mistake 89
mistake as to motive 86–7
mistake as to substantial qualities 85
mistake as to value 87–9
mistaken party
fault 90
risks 90
nature of mistake 78, 84
no knowledge of mistake 78–81, 99
non-disclosure
foreknowledge 92–3
information obtained at significant expense 91, 93
no obligation to disclose 91
personal information 91
productive information 91, 94
positive misrepresentation 89
protection of reliance 78
public knowledge 94
redistributive information 93
seriousness of mistake 84, 85
should have known of mistake 78, 82–4, 89, 90, 99
specially disadvantaged parties 87
uncertainty 84
unilateral mistake 78
pre-contract enquiries
incomplete information 25
National Conveyancing Protocols 25
property transactions 25
requirement 2
sale of businesses 25

Principles of European Contract Law (PECL)
absence of fair dealing 18
absence of good faith 18
acceptable principles 4
adaptation of contract 96–7
alternative to national laws 5
application 125
arbitration clauses 6
avoidance of contract 18, 89, 95
common ground 4
compromise position 4
damages 95
exercises in comparative law 5
fraud 126
generally 3, 5
governing law 5, 6
influence 11–12
international recognition 5
misrepresentation 16
mistake
  careless mistake 90
  fundamental mistake 85, 125
  generally 14, 16–19
  mistake as to fact 125
  mistake as to law 125
  mistake as to motive 87
  mistake as to value 88
model for development 5
non-disclosure 14, 93
protecting reasonable expectations 73
purposes 5
remedy for mistake 19
restatement 4, 6
revision 4
shared principles 4, 7
unilateral mistake 18–19
unilateral relief 72

remedies
adaptation of contract 96–7
avoidance of contract 95
breach of contract 109–10
calculation errors 96–7
damages 95–6, 98
duress 107
fraud 97, 107
innocent misrepresentation 107
mistake as to terms 96
rescission 102
restriction 97

rescission
misrepresentation 16
party given incorrect information 102

Roman law
culpa in contrahendo 56–9
error *in substantia* 53
mistake 44, 85

Rome I Regulation
applicable law 5, 9
contractual relations 5

sale of goods
duty of disclosure 21
goods fit for purpose 21, 26
goods of satisfactory quality 21, 26
implied terms 26
sale in course of business 26

sales of land
caveat emptor 26, 28
defective title 27
indirect duty to disclose 26–7
National Conveyancing Protocols 25, 27–8

unusual facts (unknown unknowns) 27–8
standard form contracts
exclusion clauses 102, 116–17
implications 100
red-hand rule 101
unfair contract terms 101–2
unfair surprise 100, 102
unusual clauses 100–1
Study Group on a European Civil Code (SGECC) 3

unconscionable bargains
conscious exploitation 23
disadvantaged claimants 23
lack of explanation 36
mistake 22–23
oppressive nature of contract 23
relief 23
special disability 23, 36
value of property 22
unfair contract terms
business to business (B2B) contracts 102, 116
excluded contracts 116
exclusion clauses 102
Law Commission 102, 105, 117, 119
procedural fairness 102
standard form contracts 100–2
UNIDROIT Principles of International Commercial Contracts (UPICC)
arbitration clauses 6

avoidance of contract 79–80
fraud 129
generally 3, 4
governing law 6
influence 11–12
mistake
definition 128
relevant mistake 128
unilateral mistake 19
protecting reasonable expectations 73
purpose 127
unilateral relief 72
United States of America
contract law
reliance 69, 80
unconscionability 69
voidable contract 70
defective property 70–1
disclosure
calculation errors 92
defective property 92
efficiency gains 94
financial services 93–4
non-disclosure 71, 93–4
mistake
bids based on mistake 69
error of judgment 70
knowledge of mistake 69
risk of mistake 70
unilateral mistake 70
voidable contract 70
State laws 68
tenders
bids based on mistake 69
reliance on bid 69
unjust enrichment
prevention 41